MW01064491

# Study Skills for College Writers

# Study Skills for College Writers

Laurie Walker
*Eastern Michigan University*

Bedford/St. Martin's    Boston • New York

Copyright © 2002 by Bedford/St. Martin's

All rights reserved.
Manufactured in the United States of America.

21 20 19 18 17
u   t   s   r   q

*For information, write:* Bedford/St. Martin's, 75 Arlington Street,
Boston, MA 02116 617-399-4000

ISBN-10: 0–312–39638–4
ISBN-13: 978–0–312–39638–1

# Preface for Instructors

When I was invited to develop a brief study skills guide for underprepared students, I eagerly jumped at the chance to share my nineteen years of experience teaching English, art, reading, and college success. Sitting squarely at the heart of this brief book is the one question that drives my professional inquiry: How do we learn best?

While the question is elementary, familiar to concerned and conscientious educators everywhere, the answer is anything but simple, or singular. How we learn best, the attitudes and practices most effective in and out of the classroom, varies from person to person. However, the best practices can be and often are identified by successful students, so I have turned primarily to those students for guidance in authoring this text.

Good students know that success happens less by chance than by design. Good students are made, not born. The beliefs and behaviors that engender success in school can be acquired — or learned — at any age. It is never too early nor too late to expand our metacognitive repertoire, to understand more about *how* we learn what we learn. Because writing well requires *thinking* well — and is only artificially separable from listening, speaking, and reading well — nearly all of what we call 'good study skills' are involved in the act. Attention to strategic, systematic, and skillful study is thus a natural complement to formal writing instruction.

There are some in higher education who believe students should know how to study long before they arrive on any college campus. I agree. Nonetheless, what students *should* know and what they *do* know do not always match, and coupling study skills instruction with writing instruction helps to remove much of the associated 'remediation' stigma.

I wrote this book because there seemed to be a need for a concise but comprehensive compilation of practical suggestions students can enact and enjoy in their quest to learn. I believe this study guide helps to meet that need. *Study Skills for College Writers* intends to provide college students and teachers with varied tools and challenges from which to pick and choose as each seeks a superior education. Topics include helpful tips and strategies for managing time, taking notes, taking tests, and using college resources. Addressing students as emerging scholars, *Study Skills for College Writers* assumes that the motivation to learn is, for most of us, as instinctive as drawing breath. It models the attitudes and behaviors that have enabled others to overcome adversity, to achieve, and to revel in learning. My hope is that you and your students will find it useful. May it provide a welcome guide to the art of study.

## ACKNOWLEDGMENTS

Many people helped to bring this book into being. I thank Ray Quiel, my Registered Domestic Partner and communications Professor extraordinare; my daughters Emily and Amanda, able learners and the light of my life; my co-author of *Right From The Start* and the Dean of Graduate Studies at EMU, Dr. Robert Holkeboer; Genevieve Hamilton, Associate Editor, for her invaluable editing skills and Michelle Clark, Editor, for the invitation to write. Thanks also to the many reviewers who contributed mightily to this effort: Susan R. Clark, Central Michigan University; Sheilah R. Craft, Marian College; Barbara Jensen, Modesto Junior College; Kaye Kolkmann, Modesto Junior College; Sandra Lakey, Pennsylvania College of Technology; Gerald T. McCarthy, San Antonio College; Sandra H. Moore, Mississippi Delta Community College; Cleatta R. Morris, Louisiana State University, Shreveport; Jeanie Page Randall, Austin Peay State University; and David Waddell, California State University, Chico. Finally, I wish to thank each of my former, present, and future students. You give me hope and teach me well.

# Contents

# — Chapter 1 —
# Your Resources: Let's Explore

Each of us has internal — or inner — resources: our interests, our desire to learn, our tolerance for uncertainty, our work ethic, our self-discipline. We have abilities, too: to visualize, to prioritize, to categorize, to reason and solve problems, to manage (or mismanage) our time, to embrace change, to exercise our imagination. Moreover, we each have specialized knowledge from our lived experience and prior learning. This specialized knowledge can perhaps be considered our most important resource.

Along with internal resources, we have external resources: the world and its inhabitants and people's inventions. The specialized knowledge others possess and are willing to share makes up the bulk of what we call our external resources. Learning is all about internalizing external resources; to make the most of both, we must begin with identification. What are the internal and external resources that you, personally, can claim? Let's explore possible answers to that question.

## INTERNAL RESOURCES

### *Getting to Know You*

- How well do you know yourself?
- Do you know your strengths and weaknesses?
- Do you know what you like and dislike?
- What gets you excited?
- Can you see where you would like to be in ten years?
- Can you define success in your own terms?

If you answered yes to most of these questions, you have what it takes to explore and to capitalize on your inner resources.

Because we grow and change throughout our lives, we may believe that we know ourselves one day and that we are second-guessing ourselves the next. This is normal — even desirable in many ways. It says we are willing to grow and change; it says we are learning. As lifelong learners, we will find that some of our interests, goals, and strengths will change over time but that many will remain constant or will deepen. As college students, we have unparalleled opportunities for self-discovery. Some of these opportunities will arise in our classroom conversations; some will arise outside of class in other conversations; most opportunities for self-growth or self-discovery, however, we must create ourselves.

So if desire is the key to self-discovery and you have the desire, let's take inventory. To identify your store of inner resources, complete each of the following exercises in turn. These simple assessment steps will boost your confidence, clarify your capabilities, and provide a plan of action to help you hit the ground running here at college.

## TRY IT!   WHAT ARE YOU GOOD AT?

What do you do better than most people? For instance, I make a mean cheesecake. I also draw a fair pencil portrait. There are many things I don't do well, but these two things I do. Write down ten conclusions to this incomplete sentence ("Watching TV" doesn't count):

I am good at _____

I am good at _____

I am good at _____

I am good at _____

I am good at _____

I am good at _____

I am good at _____

I am good at _____

I am good at _____

I am good at _____

"Study your list for a minute. Does it reflect at least some of your interests, aptitudes, abilities, or skills? Think about how these skills might help you in school. Then circle five of the ten that could each possibly lead to a major, a course of study, or a career. Next to the skill you've identified and circled, spell out the major, course of study, or career and perhaps write a sentence describing how the one leads to the other.

## TRY IT! I AM A . . . ?

In the same spirit of self-assessment and exploring inner resources, complete this incomplete sentence ten times:

I am a _____

I am a _____

I am a _____

I am a _____

I am a _____

I am a _____

I am a _____

I am a _____

I am a _____

I am a _____

For example, "I am a writer." "I am a mother." "I am a lover of nature." "I am a teacher." "I am a fan of alternative music, a hard worker, a theater enthusiast and a loyal friend." "I am a spinner of wool and a country girl (at heart and by birth)." There are my ten. After you've described yourself in this way, order your list according to the size of the group affiliation, with the largest first. I'd guess that largest group affiliations in my list would be (1) friend, (2) mother, (3) hard worker, (4) teacher, (5) writer . . . in that order. The smallest groups I affiliate with are probably spinner of wool and theater enthusiast. How about you?

The small group affiliations represent areas of our lives in which we hold specialized knowledge or expertise. On campus, online, and in our local communities, we can gather with people who share these interests. We can also share our expertise with others by teaching or tutoring. Specialized knowledge — usually born of practice, achievement, or experience — is a valid and valuable resource. Post this list to remind yourself of your talents and expertise. Then put those resources to work for you — in school and in life.

**TRY IT!  DRAW YOUR LIFE MAP**

Draw it big; fill it up. On a large poster board or piece of newsprint, record the significant events that have shaped your identity and have helped make you the person you are today. Begin by recording your date and place of birth at the top or in the upper-left-hand corner, and be sure to include people, dates, places, moves, and achievements. Depict these turning points in some way with graphic representation — a photo, a collage, a freehand sketch — starting at your birth and working your way to the present.

Keep your Life Map chronological; focus first on the most important events, then fill in the gaps. Because this is meant to be a poster, of sorts, of your life, be creative and emphasize the visual. If you have a new roommate or suitemate, make a date to do this together some night: Break out the markers and photos, the glue and whatever will stick. Hang (and admire!) your finished Life Map for at least a few days or perhaps longer, particularly if this is your first semester at college. Completing this poster will better acquaint you with the shaping events of your life and will offer a helpful biography, at a glance, for new acquaintances, roommates, and friends.

### Goals and Motivation

Your motives — your personal purposes — for going to class or staying in school will depend on your long-range goals and dreams. Academic motivation also rests heavily on your sense of the correlation between a college education and your long-range goals and dreams.

Good goals are clear and precise. They are also realistic. Dreams may let us shoot for the moon, but goals take us there one step at a time. To reach our goals consistently, it helps to spell them out — in writing — and locate these written reminders in places we visit frequently, such as our pockets (the to-do list), book bag, briefcase, daily calendar, refrigerator door, or computer screen. Whether the goal is short-term (pass this quiz) or long-term (graduate with honors), a visible, explicit reminder will increase the likelihood that it gets done.

Another way to transform intentions into accomplishments is to tell someone about your goals, preferably someone you see often or someone close to you. Ask this person to remind you (and when to remind you) of this goal. When we confide in others we feel accountable to them, not just to ourselves.

Motivation is marvelous and also necessary if we hope to achieve. Some struggle with summoning the motivation to climb out of bed each day, while others have heaps of motivation but difficulty channeling it. How can you find this force that moves you to action? Where does motivation or inspiration come from? There is no single source, of course; sources of motivation are as numerous as the stars in the sky. What serves as a motive one day might leave you listless the next; you might lose motivation today and then find it again tomorrow.

Motivation isn't so much lost and found, though, as it is made. We generate this energy just as we generate enthusiasm for our favorite teams or performers. Both the athlete and the academic know that motivation is essential to turning in a solid performance at any given moment. Tied to the body's manufacture of adrenaline and seratonin, motivation isn't entirely a head game: Body and mind must work together.

If you truly believe that success in school now will help you get where you want to go or be the person you want to be, plant that thought in your mind. If you do, motivation will find you. It is a resource that, like water, replenishes us when we are dry. And we can — we must — go to the well again and again.

## TRY IT!  WHAT ARE YOUR GOALS?

On each of three pieces of paper, record three of your current goals: one for this week, one for this semester, and one for life. Place each piece of paper in a place where you are sure to see it and where it will serve to remind you of what is important to you, of your dreams and desires.

---

**TRY IT!   BUILDING CREDENTIALS**

To help you keep track of your inner resources and present qualifications to others in polished form, start an electronic résumé-in-progress file and a hard-copy credential file (perhaps a folder or box). In both, record or store your awards, honors, and accomplishments, academic or otherwise. Begin with your high school diploma and college acceptance letter, and then work backward. Record, too, your history of employment (however insignificant the job may seem) and all volunteer work, extracurricular activities, and formal or informal memberships or group affiliations. Briefly document unusual or extraordinary experiences you have had, such as travel.

Review and update both files at least twice each semester. You don't need to be especially systematic or orderly about collecting/recording at this point: It is, after all, a work-in-progress. Just having the data in one place (or two) will give you a head start when you are ready to polish and put your qualifications in a finished form. Remember, this is no time to be modest. Your experience and accomplishments are worth acknowledging. Record them all.

---

### *Capitalizing on Inner Resources*

Once you have identified the goals and interests that motivate you, the skills and abilities you possess, and the specialized knowledge or expertise you hold, seize all opportunities to demonstrate and expand these strengths. Self-improvement requires confronting challenges, too, of course, but first favor what *comes* naturally, what you know and do well:

If you like to talk and are good at it . . .

- take small classes where conversation is encouraged.

If listening is your strong suit . . .

- you might prefer a large-lecture class format.

A student who keyboards well but struggles with chemistry could offer to do some typing for a chem-whiz friend in exchange for tutoring. If you are a people person, organize a small-group study session. Go with your strengths. Let your light shine. Use these tools — your inner resources — to excel. Your confidence and competence will soar as you do.

EXTERNAL RESOURCES

## *Exploring Your College or University*

As important as they are, our inner resources alone are not enough to ensure success in school. We must also identify and tap external resources — all the people, places, agencies, and technologies available to assist us. Every campus community has a wealth of these resources at the student's disposal. It will be up to you to locate and use these resources, but the quest can be fun and rewarding. Faculty, staff, and administrators are all there for you, as are other campus services and personnel. Everyone in the college community benefits when students succeed and feel well-served, so be assertive about seeking out the assistance you need.

Even before you enter college and begin to explore this new world, your friends, family, former teachers, and others are a valuable circle of support. Reach out and stay in touch. Phone and e-mail these people. The more people you keep in contact with, the more resources you have, and the better off you will be. Your life and learning will be enriched for having made the effort.

## *Friends*

Where would we be without friends? We'd be lost and lonely. Every friend we have is a gift — and a resource! Our friends have talents and skills we don't; we have talents and skills they don't. And we share so much with our friends: interests, secrets, stories, and laughs. Our friends are truly our peers because we see them as equals and respect their opinions, in some ways, above those of all others.

Our friends who are also college students can appreciate as can no one else the triumphs and tribulations of college life. They empathize. We share a station in life and so are allies and confidants. We call on our friends to celebrate and commiserate with us. Without friends, it is tough to have a meaningful, active social life — and humans are inherently social. We need our friends; they need us. We can never have too many.

College is where and when many form friendships that last a lifetime. The friends I made in my first few years as an undergraduate twenty-five years ago are among my nearest and dearest to this day. It isn't hard to meet people when everyone is a newcomer; each new semester, each new class offers fresh faces and potential new friends. The typical student community in any college in America is much more diverse than the typical high school population, neighborhood, or hometown. Make the most of this chance to befriend others who have had experiences very different from your own.

To have a friend, be one. Introduce yourself; ask questions. Invite a prospective new friend to eat or study with you. Attend meetings when student organizations or special-interest groups are signing up recruits. Get out, get around, get acquainted. What you learn from friends and peers in college is called the co-curriculum, and it will likely shape your life and values to a greater extent than will classroom instruction. Because success in school is important to you, however, just be sure that when you invest your time and energy in any friendship — old or new — it is with someone who supports you all the way in this goal of academic success.

## TRY IT!  MAKE NEW FRIENDS

For the next two weeks in each of your classes, make a point to speak with one classmate you have not yet met. Try to learn this person's name and something memorable about him or her. Write down the name as soon as you are able; keep your own "class list" in this way. If the class is small enough, continue until you've learned everyone's name, and perhaps a few phone numbers or e-mail addresses, too. Then get to know at least two classmates somewhat better. If possible, get together to socialize or study outside of class.

### *Family*

Your family is your premier, primary gift and resource. While you may be closer to some members than to others, chances are very good that relationships with all family members will change once you become a college student. Your growing independence and the attendant responsibility make this a time of dynamic transition. This is especially true for parent/child and sibling/sibling relationships.

To see these relationships grow stronger and deeper, be sensitive to others' needs, hopes, and fears. Keep your parents and siblings up to speed about the enormous changes taking place in your life. Invite them to visit you on campus and walk through a typical day with you. Phone home or send an e-mail when you're having a great day, not just when you're feeling blue. Keep the lines of communication open, always, and whether the support you need to succeed academically is emotional or material, be precise when you talk with family members about how they might best offer this support.

Are you an adult student with children of your own? If yes, then it is also important to talk with your kids about your academic pursuits. Bring them to school with you now and then; include them fully in this part of your life. Explain why you want to be a college student. Be assured that as you set an example of "good student" habits and behavior, your children will become better students themselves. Your kids can be a resource, too, in ways you might not suspect. For instance, I'm thinking of my daughters Emily and Amanda, ages twenty-one and twenty-three, even as I write this sentence. Emily and Amanda are my imagined audience whenever I write for college students.

## Campus Personnel

Besides your friends and family, many people on campus are there as resources, employed to serve you. They teach, mentor, tutor, assist, advise, comfort, and guide. They feed, clean, keep records, answer phones, coach, and nurse. All personnel at your school are employed in your service; you (and your education) are the reason(s) they have the jobs they do.

Take the time to acquaint yourself with some of these people and what they can do for you. Ask questions. While many student services will be advertised, others will not; your investigation can pay off. Mutual respect leads to civility and enlightenment, so remember to be respectful when you inquire and you will be respected in turn. The faculty and staff are there for you, and most will want to meet you.

## Capitalizing on External Resources

As with your internal resources, your external resources are only as valuable as you believe them to be. You won't need to avail yourself of every service offered, and even the most well-intended advice is sometimes best ignored. Nonetheless, to capitalize on the specialized knowledge of others — the tools, technology, and services available to assist you with academic success — locate these resources, and then consult and evaluate their worth.

Chapter 2 extends the discussion begun in this chapter. It offers specific, student-tested suggestions for making the most of both on-campus and community resources.

# — Chapter 2 —
# Questioning and Help-Seeking

The ability to ask ignites our love of learning. When we want to know; we question, query, inquire, and we get answers, make discoveries. Questions drive research, investigation, and data collection, all of which help us to act wisely and solve problems.

Good students ask good questions. They hone and refine their questioning skills as well. Ultimately, asking the right questions at the right times is an art form, and the practitioner is an artist with superior skill. Here, suggestions for effective questioning apply both in and out of class because opportunities to learn and grow exist everywhere.

Help-seeking, the other topic addressed in this chapter, presents a psychological hurdle for many college students. Eager to be adult, independent learners, some mistakenly regard help-seeking as a sign of weakness or admission of failure. The willingness to seek help when needed, however, almost always ensures success.

Humans are social, interdependent creatures; we need one another to survive. Beyond the need for survival, though, our lives are richer, more varied, and more rewarding when we come together — to work, to play, to help each other out. Far from being a negative behavior, seeking help is a mark of mental maturity. Plainly, it is a wise and prudent thing to do. Next we'll examine from whom to seek help, when to do it, and how to be smart about it as you enter into this, your college experience.

## HELP-SEEKING ON CAMPUS

Again, every college or university is filled with people who are employed for the primary purpose of helping you, the student, in some way. Faculty, staff, administrators, and numerous others are — or should be — at your service. This is not to say, however, that these people will come looking for you. They won't often show up at your dorm door offering to help. As an adult student, you must take the initiative to seek assistance when you need it.

Why are some students comfortable asking for help while others are not? Some feel that seeking help implies incompetence or inadequacy. Others are shy, or they don't know how or what to ask. Dr. Jan Collins-Eaglin, a help-seeking expert, says, "These are valid thoughts but not the thinking of self-regulated learners. Self-regulated learners manage their academic outcomes. These students are motivated to do well in class and are more likely to seek out help when necessary. They are aware that all students have occasional difficulty . . . when they encounter a challenge; they do something to remedy it."[1]

You, too, can be a self-regulated learner, a savvy seeker, and a successful student with just a little practice. Start by getting acquainted with people on campus before you need their help. For a complete listing of campus personnel, consult your college directory. This directory is likely available online, through your school's Web site, and in a hard-copy or phone book format. Memorize the college switchboard number, and until you know your way around campus like a scout, carry a map.

By no means complete, what follows is a list of personnel commonly found on college campuses across America:

*Administrators*
    president
    vice presidents
    provosts
    deans (academic and operational)
    directors (special programs)
    department chairs
    Board of Regents

*Faculty*
    professors
    instructors
    lecturers
    graduate student teaching assistants

*Staff (Academic)*
    advisors
    admissions officers
    financial aid officers
    registrar
    records officers
    staff assistants
    clerical workers
    student workers
    tutors

*Staff (Personal)*
    campus police
    resident advisors
    health care and fitness providers

---

[1]Elizabeth Morgan, et al., *Being, Building, Becoming* (Dubuque, Iowa: Kendall Hunt Publishing Co., 2001), p. 57.

      counselors
      physical plant engineers
      maintenance employees
      food service employees
      coaches

Although they may have different titles at your school, these people, together with you, comprise your college or university. They are your richest store of external resources. When Regis Philbin asks, "Do you want to use a lifeline?" we know what he means. A person will answer the call.

### *Student Services*

All schools have student services designed to assist you with academic success. These resources range from academic advising to health and fitness; career planning and placement to subject-specific tutoring; personal counseling, housing, the Department of Public Safety, and more. Colleges also often have services for particular populations, such as international students, nontraditional students, or students who commute. Not all services for students on or near campus are provided by the school; student-run organizations offer a rich resource, too.

Academic student services commonly include the college library, computer labs, writing labs, math labs, tutoring (both giving and receiving), and central or departmental academic advising.

Special-interest groups abound: fraternities and sororities, arts organizations, intramural athletics, philanthropic (Big Brothers, Big Sisters) government programs (ROTC, Americorps), and self-help groups. Chances are very good that if you have an area of interest (skiing? poetry? horses?) there is a like-minded group on campus. If not, find a faculty advisor and start one! Student-run organizations are encouraged by the college at large; often there is money available for startup costs.

## TRY IT! EXPLORE STUDENT SERVICES

To learn the student services and student-run organizations at your school, consult your student handbook, the student government office, or the office of campus life; ask friends, resident advisors, and instructors. The campus directory will most likely list these groups alphabetically. During orientation or registration, these organizations often recruit and distribute information. Based on your findings, check out the top two that interest you, in person and at your earliest convenience.

### TRY IT!  FIND A SPECIAL INTEREST GROUP

Call the number for campus information to inquire about a specific interest group even if you are unsure whether the group or office exists. Check out the college Web page; do a subject search. A couple well-placed inquiries are usually all you need to find out if the service or group you are looking for is out there and, if so, where (and who the contact person might be).

Evidence suggests that students who get involved with service and special interest groups do better academically than those who do not. Take advantage of these resources, but remember: Academic concerns come first. If you find your involvement in any such activity is taking up time in nonproductive ways, don't fear being a quitter. Saying no when you have good reason to do so — or feel overextended — is an assertive and wise choice.

### TIP!  THE DEAN OF STUDENTS

Your school's dean of students — or vice president of student affairs — is an important person to know. This person's job is to advocate for students. He or she investigates student complaints, runs interference, and often acts as a mediator in conflict resolution. It is a good idea to inform the dean of students if you have an accident or medical emergency that means you will miss several classes; the dean will inform your instructors. The dean of students can also refer you to the appropriate resource if he or she is unable to directly assist you with solving a problem. Call first, then stop by and meet your dean of students. Shake hands. You will be glad you did.

## HELP-SEEKING IN THE COMMUNITY

### *The World within Arm's Reach*

Beyond the campus borders there is likely a local community filled with resources well worth exploring. Whether this community is a college town, a cow town, or a big city, there will be good reason to get familiar with what is where and determine the walking or driving distance to all your life's necessities:

- Where can you get cheap gas, good food, and fairly priced, clean lodging?
- Where can you take in a movie and where is the nearest mall?
- Is there local mass transit — say, a bus route — that can get you there?
- If you live on campus, you may seek a neighborhood church to attend or a nearby bank.
- Where are the best and nearest coffee shops? copy shops? bookstores? office or art supply stores? food co-ops or farmers' markets?

A few community resources that college students are advised to locate early include the local library, post office, and clinics/hospitals. There may be local civics groups or interest groups, too, that you will want to check out. Do learn about local lore, the history or whatever it is your home-away-from-home is famous for. Visit "special" attractions unique to this area or community. Make yourself comfortable and familiar with your new environs.

## TRY IT!  INVITE A FRIEND

Because exploring is usually more fun when you do it with someone, once you have collected the requisite phone books and maps, invite a friend — old or new — to undertake a local expedition with you. Allow enough time to move about at a leisurely pace. Share your impressions and experience. Talk about what you see and do; compare reactions. Then spread the word — share your findings with others, particularly with students also new to your school.

## TRY IT!  GET TO KNOW YOUR INSTRUCTORS

Visit one — or all — of your instructors during office hours and contact one — or all — via e-mail. It is best to do this early in the term, but anytime is better than not at all. Have a specific question to pose when you visit or write, preferably one concerning course content or conduct.

### *The World beyond Arm's Reach*

Thanks to the Internet and other technological wonders that enable us to communicate with most anyone in the world at any time, it is now fair to say the entire world is seldom beyond arm's reach. Still, while you can chat online with your friend at the University of Hawaii, you can't as yet slap hands in real time if you attend Eastern Michigan University. That's OK. If we could be everywhere in the world at once, there would be no thrill in travel or seeing sites/sights previously unseen. Nonetheless, the global village is here, and it is real. The world is your oyster — and your resource — for the discovering.

Every college student, including you, has at his or her disposal access to the Internet, fax, and telephone lines. Older forms of communication circle the globe more slowly and include printed or recorded materials: books, newspapers, music. These vehicles for communication and this wealth of information are at our fingertips and are dangerous to ignore. When the world comes knocking at your door, open it. You can always close the door again when you need solitude or privacy.

## TIP!  THE INTERNET

The Internet is the world's largest computer network. It is a vast, tremendous resource connecting computer users around the globe, across space and time. The Internet is invaluable for college students, who can search databases, confer through caucus and newsgroups, chat online, share video and audio files, and read syllabi, professional journals, and literary classics. You can find an answer to almost any question you can imagine on the Internet, and the easiest available map for navigating it is the World Wide Web. Software that helps you navigate the Web (Netscape and Internet Explorer, for instance) will soon be built into all computers and televisions.

The Internet can be accessed by most college students through direct-access ports in the library, computer labs, and residence halls or by modem from home. Most colleges offer classes or workshops about Internet search strategies and evaluating the quality of Internet sites; most also offer courses conducted entirely via the Internet. If you are not yet a frequent Internet user, get on and surf! Invite a friend who is perhaps more adept to show you three or four of his or her favorite sites.

---

**TRY IT! E-MAIL A FRIEND**

Send an e-mail to a friend who attends a college or university located in another state, preferably a state you have not visited. Ask this friend to describe his or her new school for you, to tell you how it's going and what's been difficult or a pleasant surprise. Agree to exchange messages once a week if possible; strike up an e-mail-pal correspondence. Even if your messages are brief but regular, having a faithful correspondent is an uncommonly good thing. This relationship will enable you to solicit specific experiences, opinions, and perspectives from another vantage point.

---

### Help Seeking Anytime, Anywhere

We seek help or tap external resources to accomplish more, learn more, experience success. To do so effectively, we must

1. Be aware of task or assignment difficulty.
2. Consider all available, possible resources.
3. Ask for help.
4. Process the help so as to successfully complete the task.

I have often noticed that students who have no trouble accepting money for school are reluctant to ask for other kinds of help, such as tutoring in difficult subjects. Help can come in many forms and from many people in many places. Don't be discouraged if you sometimes seek help that proves fruitless; as with anything else, help-seeking requires trial and error.

I learned to ask for help early in my college career. As a young mother with small children, I was sure it would take me twenty years to graduate — unless I got help. I accepted all offers! Many people enjoy helping others, particularly when they can easily share or teach what they know or can do. Being asked validates their expertise and experience.

The benefits of help-seeking for college students include saving time, saving money, developing relationships, raising grades, graduating faster, and, finally, remembering and applying more of what you learn. This last point is important. When seeking help, do you look for a quick fix or learn how to solve the problem in a way that will enable you to solve future problems? Asking for help to learn a new skill is preferable to asking just to get the job done or to have someone do it for you. When we focus on learning in our help-seeking, we become better students.

## QUESTIONING

There are, of course, no bad questions; the only bad question is the one never asked. The best, most efficient way to get answers is to ask questions. There are, however, ways to ask more effective questions and techniques we can practice to improve our questioning abilities.

**TRY IT!   ASKING GOOD QUESTIONS**

How can you know when or if you are asking good questions? Take stock by answering the following as honestly as possible:

1. Do you ask questions when you have them?
2. In class, during a lecture, discussion, or test, do you ask the instructor to clarify information if you are confused or unclear about anything?
3. In conversation, if someone uses a word that is new to you, do you ask what the word means?
4. Do you ever ask a classmate to swap notes or to do homework or study with you?
5. When meeting someone for the first time, do you ask questions to get acquainted?
6. Do you rephrase questions and pose them again in slightly different form if they do not yield a satisfactory response the first time?
7. When asking someone a question, do you allow him or her sufficient thought time (three to five seconds) to respond?
8. Do you ever write down mock exam questions to guide your test preparation or study?
9. Do you write down questions that occur to you when taking notes during a lecture? when reading?
10. Do you ever approach your instructor after class or during office hours with questions?

If you answered yes to five or fewer of these questions, your questioning practices will benefit by attention, and in the ways described. Unless you answered yes to all of the preceding ten questions, the following discussion should be helpful for you.

## *Asking the Right Questions*

Questioning is key to learning. As with help-seeking (and a vital part of help-seeking), the willingness to risk a question is one behavior that sets successful students apart from unsuccessful students. Because we are life-long learners whether in the classroom or elsewhere, asking the right question of the right person (or persons) at the right time is how we gather information and become knowledgeable.

"But," you ask, "what is the right question?" There's the rub. Your purpose for asking, who you ask, and the context in which you ask will determine how "right" the question is or isn't. The right questions are not necessarily those that produce the expected response. Rather, the right questions — much like planting good seed in good soil — produce beyond expectation, yielding a rich return.

Often — not always, but often — the right question

- Leads to other questions, becomes a series rather than a single query.
- Cannot be answered on the spot. It requires research, a little time and investigation, to answer.
- Is open-ended, yields an expansive rather than a yes or no response. (e.g., "What are you doing right now?" instead of "Are you doing something right now?")
- Sparks conversation, fuels dialogue, inspires thought.
- Is controversial.
- Feels risky.
- Is clearly phrased.
- Is addressed to more than one person.
- Is a question you have asked before.

Few two-year-olds have trouble asking questions. At two, if we want to know why the sky is blue, we say, "Why is the sky blue?" Then, if we don't get a satisfactory answer, we keep asking our questions — seeking, searching — sometimes right into adulthood or until we do get an acceptable response. Children have a seemingly insatiable, innate curiosity. Curiously, though, some of us lose this childlike sense of wonder as we age and find that asking becomes more difficult.

Especially as students, if our questions were ever ridiculed or ignored, we may have learned to silence ourselves and our questions as a defense mechanism, as an ego-protection strategy. The good news is that we can un-learn this habit, too, and regain that childlike love of learning if we are willing to try. Remember: There are no bad questions, no dumb questions. There are only asked and unasked, answered and unanswered questions.

## *Questioning in Class*

Formulating good questions in class is, in large measure, a listening skill. An active, comprehensive listener seeks to understand the speaker, just as an active, comprehensive reader seeks to understand the author. Because both senders and receivers share responsibility for communication or meaning-making, forming and posing good questions — then having them addressed — increases understanding for all parties involved. In the classroom, this means that you, your classmates, and your teacher all benefit when you ask a question.

Once we have embraced the willingness to ask questions, we must learn when, what, where, why, who, how, and how often to ask. Listening experts Andrew Wolvin and Carolyn Gwynn Coakley suggest that, while in class, we should try to do the following:

- **Wait until the speaker has completed his or her message before asking questions.** Often we interrupt to question prematurely. If patient, our questions may be answered in the course of the lecture.
- **Avoid interruption during a speaker's address.** If it is imperative to interrupt, do so politely. Raise a hand.
- **Do not ask questions that are irrelevant, distracting, or only marginally related to the topic at hand.** Instead, write these questions down in your notes and ask them after class or after the address.
- **Attend to the tone of your questions. Avoid sarcasm, skepticism, and hostility when questioning.** A judgmental, condescending, or angry tone makes speakers defensive and inhibits clear communication, comprehension, and understanding.
- **Avoid loaded or rhetorical questions, which seem insincere and judgmental.** Loaded questions begin with faulty assumptions (e.g., "When are we meeting tomorrow?"), whereas rhetorical questions answer themselves (e.g., "None of you has any questions, do you?").
- **Be willing to listen to the answers to our questions.** Even if we disagree or find those answers longer than anticipated, it is better to listen to the answer before we question.
- **Check understanding frequently.** This can take the form of paraphrasing and restating the response to our questions or of careful note-taking and instructor/speaker review of those notes.

### IN SUM

Questioning and help-seeking ensure student success. Effective learners ask questions, and they ask for help assertively. Because questioning is a big part of gathering and evaluating information, of listening and note-taking, and of reading and writing, it will be a skill featured in the "Try It!" suggestions throughout the coming chapters.

# — Chapter 3 —
# Time Management

The Beatles sang, "All you need is love." My students say, "All I need is time." Time is the great equalizer: We each have twenty-four hours in a day, seven days each week, three hundred and sixty-five days per year. True, we won't all have the same number of days, weeks, or years; however, for the duration of our days on earth, time will be meted out in equal measure. How you choose to use yours sets you apart from the next person; these choices, then, ensure your individuality.

It is crucial to our health and well-being to feel we control the clock and not that the clock controls us. And so we seek to manage our time, take charge, seize the day. Effective time management means prioritizing and learning to schedule. Effective time management reduces stress, alleviates anxiety, and increases efficiency and productivity. It also enables us to enjoy our lives — this precious resource we call time — in full measure.

MAKING TIME FOR . . .

## Goals

Your short- and long-term goals will govern how you use your time, will show if you are focused and driven to accomplish those goals. Even when you change your mind and therefore change your goals, having articulated — spelled out — goals can help you spend time in satisfying ways. You probably have educational goals (ace this class, graduate in five years), career goals (own my own business), and personal and family goals (two children, two dogs, summers at the seashore). All of your goals are linked, however, by your priorities and values, and they are linked past to present to future, across time.

## Priorities and Values

We make priorities of what we value; then we allocate our time accordingly. If you are an older, returning student and a parent, chances are good that caring for your child or children is a priority. On the other hand, if you are eighteen and childless, your priorities will be quite different.

Values are choices. They are also beliefs that guide our choices. Some people place great value on a college education; others, almost none.

Each of us enters college with a well-developed set of values — values shaped by parents, friends, employers, teachers, work, school, our communities, the media, the culture, and our experiences. To feel that we are living rightly or using our time in the best possible ways, our goals should be consistent with our priorities and values.

Sometimes we need to clarify our values, or what is important to us, and the time spent doing this is well spent. It can save time later on. If your current time-management practices leave you feeling rushed, frazzled, or bored, take charge and control your clock. Don't let the clock control you. The first step toward this goal is to know what you do value.

## TRY IT!    WHAT DO YOU VALUE?

Your values will change over time; some will fade, and others will grow stronger. You will become more convinced about some things and less so about others. A passion for the piano at age eight may taper off slowly; conversely, it may lead to a career as a concert pianist.

Review the following, and then add three to the list. Rank each from 1 to 12, with 1 being your highest priority and 12 your lowest:

| | |
|---|---|
| education | _____ |
| self-improvement | _____ |
| having a mate | _____ |
| meaningful work | _____ |
| helping others | _____ |
| friends | _____ |
| happiness | _____ |
| family | _____ |
| health | _____ |
| _____ | _____ |
| _____ | _____ |
| _____ | _____ |

Your top-five values are your current priorities. Are your goals in line with these priorities? Are you allocating your time accordingly? Take stock.

---

### TRY IT!　WHERE WILL YOU BE?

Describe a typical day in your life ten years from now. Where will you be, and what will you do? Who will be there with you? Detail the whole day, hour by hour. If sufficiently detailed, this description will help you link your current uses of time with your long-term goals.

---

## SCHEDULING

Schedules are tools that help us accomplish goals. A class schedule moves you toward your degree, whereas a work schedule helps pay the bills. Effective time management requires active involvement with scheduling; it is your time, your clock, your life — and you want to make the most of it.

College students — or adults in general — have more choice, more voice, and ultimately more control about how they use their time than do younger people, even though this may not always seem the case. With this increasing freedom, too, comes responsibility and accountability — two true hallmarks of independence.

What can a schedule do for you? It can get you started, regulate daily living, foster good habits, reduce stress, and increase efficiency and productivity. A schedule provides a plan, frees the mind, and enables greater enjoyment of discretionary time. Often, effective scheduling actually creates discretionary time. By serving to remind us of due dates, tasks, events, and commitments, schedules free up brain space so that we can think about other things. It is easier to focus on English in your English class, for example, if you are not preoccupied with trying to remember where Jill plans to meet you for lunch. (See Appendix 1 for a sample schedule.)

### Daily and Weekly Schedules

The best schedules are written reminders that travel where we do. That is why a date book — or daily planner — is the top tool of the time-management trade. Daily or weekly planners come in all shapes, sizes, and formats, including electronic "pocket" organizers. Shop around a bit to find the one that is right for you. If you've never used a planner before, it may take a while to become accustomed to consulting it regularly. Don't fret if your first few attempts to use this tool are imperfect — it takes time to learn new routines, new habits, and organizational skills. Keep at it. Tell yourself to consult and record in your planner at least twice a day, first thing in the morning and last thing at night. Carve out a good half-hour (say, every Sunday evening) to record plans for the week ahead. And carry your daily planner with you every day!

What should you record? Start with due dates for school projects, tests, presentations, and papers. Record important meetings and appointments and when bills are due. If you have a work schedule that changes week to week, record your work schedule, special events you plan to attend (concerts, weddings), and other commitments. Record progress toward a goal or cross out tasks accomplished. Done! (That felt great, didn't it?)

Some people find that keeping a separate to-do list for lower-priority items helps with deciding what to do first. For instance, sending e-mail to a friend or a card to Aunt Evelyn for her birthday are less important than studying for your physics test. If you keep high- and lower-priority items on separate lists, you can consult the latter when you have finished the former. Sending a card to your aunt will feel more like play than work if you have attended to first things first.

### Monthly, Semester, and Yearly Schedules

Post a calendar in a prominent place where you stay or live. On it, record reminders for yourself AND for those who live with you. If your girlfriend is coming to campus this weekend, for instance, your roommate will appreciate the reminder. Some students post copies of their syllabi for any given semester with significant due dates highlighted. Again, try out a few different forms of "posted" schedules to see what works best for you. The trick to this form of time management is to make your reminders visual and unavoidable. Having lists, clocks, watches, and calendars nearby promotes frequent inspection.

A wall or desk calendar is useful for noting long-range goals and plans, seeing the big picture at a glance. If your long-term goals seem daunting ("read *Moby-Dick* by April"?!), break them into smaller chunks or tasks that seem less daunting ("read forty pages each week"). You may be surprised at how painless the seemingly impossible is to accomplish when you chip away at it little by little. Along with informing ourselves of the contours of our month, semester, or year up ahead, calendars, like bulletin boards or designated posting places, improve communication among people who share living quarters.

**TRY IT!   WHAT'S YOUR SCHEDULE?**

On the following page, mock up a weekly schedule for next semester that represents an improvement over your present weekly schedule. Block time for eating, sleeping, socializing, exercising, studying, attending classes, and working at your job — all the needs you anticipate. Be realistic but hopeful. If you currently attend classes four days each week and would prefer all Tuesday/Thursday classes, see if that can be done. Consider what works and what doesn't with your current schedule. Assess the pros and cons of dropping or adding commitments.

Know your limits. Strive for balance in the type of classes or activities you take on. Don't overload yourself, but don't underload yourself either. A class that meets once a week may sound appealing just now, but if you need more frequent contact, you may struggle to keep up. Think it through. Schedule carefully, and your days will be more carefree. That's the beauty and benefit of taking time to plan.

**TIP!   SCHEDULING FOR SUCCESS**

Here are fifteen suggestions for effective time management:

1. Think about your use of time; make it a priority.
2. Purchase and use a daily/weekly planner.
3. Post calendars and syllabi.
4. Wear or carry a watch.
5. Designate the same one-half hour each week to plan for the coming week.
6. Schedule blocks of time for big projects.
7. Expect the unexpected.
8. Overestimate the time you will need for specific tasks.
9. Schedule breaks and downtime.
10. Don't confuse faster with better.
11. Make to-do lists.
12. Learn to say no.
13. Ignore the negativity and harsh judgments of others.
14. Be flexible.
15. Be persistent.

# Weekly Schedule

| 7:00 AM | Monday | Tuesday | Wednesday | Thursday | Friday | Saturday | Sunday |
|---------|--------|---------|-----------|----------|--------|----------|--------|
| 8:00 | | | | | | | |
| 9:00 | | | | | | | |
| 10:00 | | | | | | | |
| 11:00 | | | | | | | |
| Noon | | | | | | | |
| 1:00 PM | | | | | | | |
| 2:00 | | | | | | | |
| 3:00 | | | | | | | |
| 4:00 | | | | | | | |
| 5:00 | | | | | | | |
| 6:00 | | | | | | | |
| 7:00 | | | | | | | |
| 8:00 | | | | | | | |
| 9:00 | | | | | | | |
| 10:00 | | | | | | | |

## TAKING CHARGE

According to management expert Peter Drucker, "It's more important to do the right things than to do things right." You may agree; you may disagree. Only you, however, can determine what those "right things" are. Likewise, only you can assess — or change — your use of time. Attempting to fulfill someone else's agenda is a sure prescription for disaster. Live your life on your own terms and spend your time as you choose. If your values are praiseworthy, your life will be, too.

There are, however, some occasions when the unexpected upsets our best-laid plans. Seldom do we plan to have a flat tire on the way to class. A bout with the flu will slow you down, as will stress of any sort. Still, there are ways to take charge of your time once more, to overcome detours and obstacles and get back on the path you have set for yourself.

Two ways to do this are as follows. First, know your personal peak times and identify troublesome time-wasters. Second, make no excuses and banish procrastination, now and forever, from your repertoire of time-management practices.

### Peak Times and Time-Wasters

Just as each of us spends time in ways we don't always feel good about, we each have personal, peak-performance times, too. It is wise to schedule your high-priority tasks for times you are likely to be at your best. If you've never been a morning person, for instance, don't sign up for 8 a.m. classes! If you are generally at your best in the early afternoon, tackle your most important or difficult work then.

One common strategy for avoiding a task is to imagine it as an unpleasant one. We talk ourselves into putting off that essay assignment until the last minute because we believe it will be drudgery — and so it will. Engaging in negative self-talk is a time-waster. It makes work expand to fill the time available for its completion. If you have had that essay assignment for two weeks, it has taken you two weeks to complete what might have been done in three hours two weeks earlier. A better approach is to practice positive self-talk — and to reward yourself for even small accomplishments.

One person's waste of time is another's golden moment. If you dislike reading, spending your morning curled up with a cup of tea and a book might sound like torture. To me, it sounds like Utopia. Again, if you want to use your days in ways that seem most right for you, start by identifying your current most/least fulfilling uses of time.

## TRY IT! HOW DO YOU SPEND YOUR TIME?

To get a handle on what your current most/least fulfilling uses of time are, chart (record) how you spend every hour of every day for three consecutive weekdays. Keep this as a written log or computer file. This task may seem tedious, at first, but if you do it diligently, you will have amassed data you can work with.

After three days, reflect on this record. Study it. Do you see any patterns of behavior? For instance, do you routinely skip lunch, then feel like a slug in the late afternoon? Are you doing well in your 1 p.m. class? If yes, perhaps this is a peak time. On this record, circle at least one hour of every day that you feel was well spent. Cross out one hour each day that you believe could have been better spent and write in how you would rather have allocated that time.

## TRY IT! TIME-WASTERS

Although peak times and wasted times are highly personal, there are some tendencies we share when it comes to feeling controlled by our clocks instead of the other way around. Highlight or check any of the following behaviors that are sometimes problematic for you:

| | |
|---|---|
| disorganization | _____ |
| overcommitting | _____ |
| negative self-talk | _____ |
| watching too much TV | _____ |
| perfectionism | _____ |
| procrastination | _____ |
| poor planning | _____ |
| unable to delegate | _____ |
| unable to say no | _____ |
| distractions | _____ |

By identifying those tendencies that sometimes lead you to spend your time unproductively, you are halfway to overcoming them. Once you've located these time-wasters, focus on ways of changing your behavior so that you are spending your time in the most productive way possible.

## *Procrastination*

Beating procrastination is a matter of mind over matter. If you know the situations in which (or the tasks at which) you habitually procrastinate, you have a head start at slaying this time-absorbing demon. Take a minute to write down three things you tend to put off:

1) _____
2) _____
3) _____

Now consider this your "hit list." You can disarm this foe!

Occasionally, procrastinating can seem advantageous: Put off taking the trash out and someone else may do it for you. Avoid calling your mom and mom will eventually call you. Even these seeming resolutions, though, have hidden costs: Resentment builds; you get labeled a slacker. In truth, procrastination seldom benefits anyone. That two-page paper comes to seem monumental in your mind. Small tasks snowball, and what could have been attended to easily, immediately, acquires the appearance of something much more difficult.

Nearly everyone procrastinates now and then. To beat this bad habit, however, we must first confront it. Next, we can take a tip — or several — from the experts, offered below, and take action. Procrastination isn't inevitable.

---

### TIP!  STOP STALLING!

Here are some things you can do to take action and improve efficiency:

- Prioritize.
- Group similar tasks (make several phone calls in one sitting; run several errands with one drive around town).
- Break up large jobs into smaller chunks or steps.
- Minimize distractions (both internal and external): If you are hungry, eat; if it is noisy, find a quieter spot.
- Exhaust your excuses.
- Set reasonable goals.
- Delegate.
- Ask for help.
- Tell someone your intentions or plans.
- Post written reminders.
- Keep to your schedule.
- Make a start.
- Do it now!

## CONTROLLING YOUR CLOCK

The Scouts of America know the value of "being prepared." When it comes to effectively managing time, college students, too, might adopt this motto. A schedule will get you started, and your motives and goals will keep you going. When the unexpected happens, though, don't be thrown off course for long. Carry work with you. Study between, before, and after classes. Practice your Spanish or listen to books-on-tape for your literature class while you commute or wash dishes. Recite definitions and dates as you exercise; prepare ahead for hectic periods of the day.

Know your personal high- and low-energy times and schedule accordingly. Do the same things at the same times of day to establish order and a routine. For instance, eating and sleeping at roughly the same times each day improves and maintains stamina and energy. Minimize distractions. Overestimate the time you will need. Stop procrastinating. Say no when necessary.

The adage "work before play" goes a long way toward helping us take control of our clocks and to use our time productively. If we feel we have earned it, if we have completed our tasks, then the time we spend playing will restore and recharge; it will improve our health and general disposition. Time is a priceless resource. College can be a great time in your life and a great time to hone the practices that help you make the most of this priceless resource.

# — Chapter 4 —
# Gathering and Evaluating Information

What is information? Where is it? How do I find it? We don't have to look far for information; it surrounds us every day, every way. Information is the raw data our senses see, touch, taste, smell, and hear; it is the very stuff of life. Making sense of that raw data is our larger task: How do we sort, sift, interpret, or apply it?

This chapter examines both academic and nonacademic sources of information, means of gathering information, and tools for evaluating information. We'll consider ways to transform information into evidence, separate useful from useless information, and establish criteria for determining worth. Finally, we'll look at applying these criteria to the information that surrounds us to better communicate and improve our lives and world.

## SOURCES OF INFORMATION

### *Primary and Secondary*

Every source is a resource, so every resource (friends, family, campus personnel) can offer information. The physical world also yields up information at every turn, as does the mass media. Conventional academic sources include the Internet, the library, and field research. Usually, however, whether conventionally academic or not, a source is a person or a group of people. Sometimes you yourself are that person; frequently our sources are other people.

A source is either **primary** or **secondary.** A primary source lives the experience, conducts the experiment or interview, and observes, records, and reports findings. A secondary source reports "secondhand" the experience of another and passes along prior research.

A primary source has less distance between herself and the information than does a secondary source. For this reason, primary sources are preferred; generally, they are more compelling and credible than secondary sources. If your English instructor tells you what she has published, that's primary information. If a classmate tells you what your English instructor has published, that's secondary information. You are the primary source for your own experience, and that experience is every bit as valid as that of anyone else!

Whether our source is primary or secondary, academic or nonaca-demic, we must identify that source before we can tap it and gather the information we seek. Next, it is necessary to determine how best to use the information obtained, or whether to use it at all. For more sugges-tions regarding source location and use, consult your composition handbook's research section, your reference librarian, or your instructor.

## TRY IT!  GENERATING SOURCES

List possible sources for the topics below. In other words, under each topic, write down all the people or places you can think of where you are likely to get useful information. List at least five likely sources — on or off campus — for each, and then put stars next to the two most accessible (and most primary) sources named on each list. Next, write down three topics important to you just now — subjects you want to know more about. Generate possible sources of information for these topics, too.

| *Transportation* | *Financial Aid* | *Writing* |
| --- | --- | --- |
| _____ | _____ | _____ |
| _____ | _____ | _____ |
| _____ | _____ | _____ |
| _____ | _____ | _____ |

| *Your Topic 1* | *Your Topic 2* | *Your Topic 3* |
| --- | --- | --- |
| _____ | _____ | _____ |
| _____ | _____ | _____ |
| _____ | _____ | _____ |
| _____ | _____ | _____ |

## MASS MEDIA MADNESS

Movies. TV. En Vogue. Drew Carey. The Dixie Chicks. The Internet. The mass media may very well be the glue that holds America together. Our fondness for pop culture eclipses other, more mundane sources of infor-mation; sometimes we must remind ourselves that it isn't the *only* source. Still, we love our movies and music, our C-span and MTV. We love the mass media in large measure because it is cheap and readily available. To turn on the radio, television, or computer requires little effort on our part. Because the broadcast media is so accessible and omnipresent, however, it is easy to become complacent, and lazy, about evaluating it.

All broadcast information, whether presented as fact or opinion, comes complete with an editorial slant, a point of view. Determining *whose* point of view can be a challenge though. Detecting bias in a newscast, for example, is difficult because the reporter is so obviously a secondary, not the primary, source. What makes it to the airwaves or an Internet site and what doesn't reveals an editing (selection) process; some of the day's events are deemed newsworthy and some are not. In short, we tend to believe — and accept as truth — what we see and hear broadcast more readily than we perhaps should. The truth, validity, and reliability of information that comes to us via the mass media must be questioned, or tested, before we can call it good information.

Your mother may tell you, "TV kills brain cells," while you find television a harmless, stress-reducing diversion. No matter what your present relationship with this source of information, in your personal quest for knowledge and truth, make sure it is only one source. Aim for balance. Tap a variety of sources: read, converse, observe. Wide-ranging investigation will provide a broader knowledge base and a bigger picture than will reliance on the mass media alone.

---

**TRY IT!  EVALUATE THE MEDIA**

Go online to at least three different newspaper Web sites (e.g., the *New York Times* [http://www.newyorktimes.com], the *Miami Herald* [http://www.miamiherald.com], and the *Los Angeles Times* [http://www.latimes.com]). Pick a current event that all three papers report. Now, carefully compare how each of the three papers describes the event. Do you see any differences in coverage? How does each newspaper write about the event? List three major differences that you see.

---

GATHERING INFORMATION

*The Evidence of Our Senses*

You've identified possible and probable sources and resources. Now what? You know what you don't know or want to learn more about: What next? This is where the hunting and gathering, the collection process comes in. Once information is located, especially if from varied sources, it must be pulled together — then evaluated. This sorting and sifting, or gathering, precedes the decision to use or act upon the information at hand.

Good methods of gathering information include using ALL our senses: taste, touch, sight, smell, and sound. In schools, sight and sound have historically been privileged above the other three, but we remember best data that engages many of these senses at once.

Trust the evidence of your senses and record as much of it as you can. Compensate for the weaknesses of one with the strengths of another. If you don't hear that well, draw the world around you. If you are "visually challenged" but hear everything, carry a small tape-recorder. The only way we can process information at all is through one or more of these senses. The more, the better. We remember vividly what we see and hear, touch and smell. Cultivate a sensitivity to the world, and from the abundance of information it provides, you will be able to selectively attend.

### A Student Writer's Resources

All students (or writers or knowledge seekers) have five primary means of gathering information, or raw data. These are

1. Observation
2. Conversation
3. Reading (and broadcast media)
4. Lived experience (or memory)
5. Imagination

Young students tend to regard imagination as the most promising means, whereas much older students invariably say memory is the richest resource. The college students I have polled say observation and conversation run a dead heat as the "most promising tools for gathering information" offered here. Finally, of all those I have talked with about this, graduate students and teachers alone claim reading as Number 1 among these five.

What does this mean? For starters, it may mean our preferred ways of gathering data are tied to development: As we grow, so does our repertoire of tools with which to learn. The trick in college, as students, is to hang on to the old ways while we try out the new, to not let imagination take a permanent backseat, for instance, to lived experience.

## TRY IT!   EXERCISE YOUR SENSES

When you set out to gather information with which to write an essay or make a presentation, try out each of these: **observe, converse, read, remember,** and **imagine.** For practice using one particular data-gathering tool at a time, try the following activities:

**OBSERVE.** Sit down in a public place and describe in writing for ten minutes where you are, who is there, and what is going on. Be specific and detailed. Fill at least one page or one screen with your observations.

**CONVERSE.** For ten to fifteen minutes, talk with a friend about the writing assignment you are currently working on in your English (or any other) class. Tape-record or take notes during this conversation; solicit suggestions from your friend about topics or approaches you might use to complete the assignment. Ask your friend to review your record of this conversation and add to or modify it for clarity and accuracy.

**READ.** Respond to a letter to the editor in today's local or school newspaper. Do you agree with the author's position? Do you disagree? Say why. Write your response for a minimum of five minutes. When finished, read aloud what you have written. OR: Enter into an online conversation with several classmates. Discuss the material you are reading for this particular class. If your instructor has not established an online venue for this purpose, invite him or her to join yours.

**REMEMBER.** In writing, tell about a time you got into big trouble or a time you were truly proud of yourself. Tell the story of a scar — any scar — on your body. Fill at least one page or two.

**IMAGINE.** Describe your ideal day, date, school, or mate. What would be perfect? Tap your imagination and write for five minutes.

The preceding means of gathering information complement what is perhaps an even more primary group of abilities: the language acts or language arts. These include listening, speaking, reading, and writing — abilities that enable us to both gather and process language-based information. Chapters 5 and 6 offer solid suggestions for strengthening our facility with these language arts.

## Inquiry and Investigation

Another word for gathering data or information is *investigation*. Journalists investigate, detectives investigate, and good writers and stellar students investigate, too. The best investigators are also skilled at inquiry: They ask the right questions at the right times.

How can you know the right question or the right time? (For more on this topic, see Chapter 2.) For now, it will help to remember that open-ended questions yield more complete, comprehensive responses (information) than do questions that can be answered "yes" or "no." To say "How are you feeling today?" will elicit a fuller response than will "Are you feeling OK today?"

Journalists query any subject with a set of stock question openers: Who? What? Where? When? Why? How? If you are stuck for a place to begin with data-gathering, try posing a question that opens with one of these words. Let's say a guest speaker is coming to campus and you have been asked to write a profile of this person and preview his or her visit for your school newspaper. Your queries might sound like this:

Who is this person?

Where is she/he from?

Why is she/he coming?

When will she/he speak to students?

Where will she/he speak to students?

What is to be the topic of his/her address?

How does this topic affect students?

What are students likely to benefit from attending?

By definition, asking questions means you seek information. And the more questions you ask, the more information you will get. The next time you ask a question, pay attention to its form. Ask more open-ended than closed questions and vary their form. If you are eagerly investigating, take care that you allow your respondent to answer each of your questions fully before asking another.

## TIP!  STORING AND RETRIEVING DATA

Effective storage and retrieval happens with good organizational skills, but you don't have to be a neat freak or wizard to develop these habits. Keeping like with like is a key concept, as is efficient use of space. What follows are some tips on how to keep the data or information you collect stored in a way (or ways) that enable easy access and retrieval.

• Keep separate folders for separate classes, but keep all class folders together in one book bag or carrying case.

• Store your books altogether, too, on one or two bookshelves, rather than having them scattered about.

• Give your computer files similar names or keep them in designated folders (e.g., "Letters" or "Psychology 101"). Having like information grouped together will lend even your piles — or room or desktop — a semblance of order.

• Take space into consideration: Do you really need all this mail or e-mail? Is it cluttering your life? If yes, purge and delete.

• Recycle old newspapers and magazines. For books you doubt you'll read again, pass them along to a friend who might appreciate them.

• Create a directory (or use the bookmark feature) for frequently visited Web sites or e-mail addresses.

When it comes to storing and retrieving information, nothing can compare with the capacity or efficiency of a microchip or hard drive. Do be sure to back up all information on your hard drive, though, when you are using CDs, disks, or paper copies. This is vital. When it comes to information, more is generally better than less. Too much information is exactly that, however, and can overload our brains with excessive detail. It also makes the process of deciding what information is useful and what useless more difficult than it needs to be.

## EVALUATING INFORMATION

### *Useful versus Useless Information*

Some information is useful and some is not. Those classified ads from last winter are definitely old news. Your teacher using a personal example to illustrate a point may be hoping you remember the point more than the personal example. In the context of learning and living day to day, we are bombarded by information and cannot possibly attend to all of it all the time. We must selectively attend. We must decide what's important for our purposes at the moment and block out other stimuli, or we won't be able to act.

To avoid experiencing "analysis paralysis" in the face of too much information, it helps to hone our skill at evaluating the usefulness of that information. We do this, in part, by establishing criteria for determining worth.

## Establishing Criteria

Criteria are the standards by which we judge the quality, value, or utility of anything. It could be the food we eat, the books we read, the movies we watch. It could be a performance. It could be information. Our standards or criteria will vary with personal preference, but three common criteria for evaluating information are

1. source credibility
2. validity
3. reliability

A source is credible if he or she is trustworthy, honest, and knowledgeable. We believe sources who have told us the truth before and have experience with the subjects about which they speak or write. We do not believe those who have lied to us in the past or offer information (opinions) on subjects they know nothing about. Primary sources tend to be more credible than secondary; paid endorsers (think TV ads) are the least credible.

Another factor that influences, heavily, our evaluation of a source's credibility is the natural bias he or she may have. To the extent that bias can be acknowledged, it should be; a neutral source may be the most desirable but the hardest to come by. Think about who wants to prove what. For example, the president of General Motors wants to sell cars; she or he has a natural bias toward "proving" GM cars are the best available. Identify bias when possible. If you want good information, you must get it from a credible source.

Validity and reliability are also criteria for evaluating information. A statement is valid if it is true or factual; it is reliable if it can be verified or replicated. A reliable car starts every time, and reliable information withstands scrutiny. If verified by another source, it remains unchanged. Any "source" who knows me will tell you my name is Laurie: That is valid and reliable information.

## *Testing Criteria*

As communicators, we evaluate information before deciding to use it as evidence in support of a thesis, position, or core claim. For example, I read in the newspaper that drug use is down in my hometown; however, this appears on the opinion page. Before I use this information to support my argument, I'd best test it and its source to determine accuracy.

Here are five questions (criteria or tests) worth applying to any information you hope to use as evidence in building an argument or case. Ask yourself:

1. Is this information recent?
2. Is it primary?
3. Is it necessary?
4. Is it sufficient?
5. Is it representative?

New information displaces old, especially in fields like technology and medicine. Be sure your information is up to date. Primary evidence is best, but is this information at all necessary? Sometimes two examples are sufficient and three are overkill. Finally, if you make general claims for a group based on individual examples, be sure these individuals are representative (typical) of the larger group. Applying these tests to raw data will allow you to assuredly use that data as evidence when you write or speak to inform or persuade an audience.

---

### TRY IT! TEST YOUR EVIDENCE

With your next assignment that requires you to use evidence drawn from sources, apply the five tests of evidence listed above. If you can answer yes to four of the five tests, use what you have with confidence. If not, keep looking for better information/evidence.

---

## COMMUNICATING INFORMATION

After we have gathered and evaluated information, synthesized and analyzed, sorted and sifted, we have undoubtedly expanded our own store of knowledge in the process. It is our turn, then, to share with others what we have learned, and we do this by communicating.

In college and in the workplace, communication usually occurs through writing and reading, speaking and listening. The next two chapters offer a wealth of ways for you to enhance your abilities to communicate, and retain, information.

# — Chapter 5 —
# Reading, Writing, and Remembering

Reading, writing, and remembering are inextricably linked activities. Without recall, we can hardly be said to be reading at all. Reading requires recollection, which requires comprehension, and comprehension often requires us to write in response to what we read.

We read differently for different purposes. If my purpose is to find a phone number, I quickly *scan* the page. I *skim* through the newspaper, reading headlines, to determine which articles I'll read more carefully and in what order. I read windows on my computer screen in a much different manner than I do textbooks; I read books with pictures differently from the way I do books without pictures. In short, my reading methods have grown more varied, flexible, and evolved over time, as my needs and interests have evolved and the methods of text delivery have changed.

To be strong readers, we must vary our approach, according to the purpose for which we're reading at the time, the rhetorical context (situation), and the type of text we're reading. A good goal for college students is to be strategic readers. As with strategic note-taking, flexibility is key.

Following this introduction are steps we can take to become better readers and to remember more of what we read. The first step is to get ready, to prepare. The second step is to use Power Reading or SQ3R strategies — approaches that emphasize goals of understanding and remembering more than speed. Comprehension, recollection, and review follow naturally from strategic reading when we are fully engaged with that reading.

A third step, writing — even briefly — in response to reading helps us stay engaged. We write for many reasons: to question, to discover what we think and feel, to enter into a dialogue with the author, to agree or disagree; we write to paraphrase, summarize, and record — all of which aid memory. Reading, writing, and remembering are the acts of true scholarship. Here are some suggestions to get you started on your journey to being that true scholar.

## STRATEGIC READING

A strategic reader knows what he or she wants to accomplish in any given reading stint. If I am strategic, I have a plan of action, a goal, and the proper tools and mindset to accomplish my purpose. College students often read for purposes of study, to learn from what they read and re-member what they learn. Reading-to-learn and learning-to-read go hand in hand; process and purpose complement each other. We constantly learn new strategies as secondary outcomes when we are reading for the primary purpose of gaining knowledge.

The two types of prose students most commonly read for purposes of study are expository (to expose, show) and narrative (to tell). Narra-tive prose characterizes text in the humanities; expository prose domi-nates the sciences. Because students have repeatedly told me that they have more trouble comprehending and retaining expository prose, we'll focus our discussion here on strategies for strengthening this type of textbook reading.

Two strategic approaches that are effective for expository textbook reading are Power Reading and SQ3R. Each involves several steps and requires the willingness to experiment and take action.

## Power Reading

### Before: Preview, Anticipate, and Question

Power Reading begins with an assignment, such as "read Chapter 10," or an objective, such as "understand conditioned response." Power Read-ing works best with expository text and for purposes of study or test preparation; it is a slow, methodical approach that does not emphasize speed. When the goal is speed, comprehension is invariably sacrificed. If you want to understand and remember what you read, speed is not your friend.

Once you have an assignment or objective, set a goal for each read-ing stint. Tell yourself you will read for thirty minutes, for instance, or until you have finished fifteen pages. Make your goals realistic; set ones you can keep. If you know you can't sit for an hour or will likely fall asleep, don't set yourself up for failure. Break your reading into manage-able chunks of time and effort. Then persevere until you reach your goal.

Next, get ready to read. Find a quiet place, minimize distraction, and sharpen your pencil. Be sure you have adequate light and heat and that you're comfortable but not too comfortable. Avoid reading in places — such as your bed or in front of the TV — that you associate most strongly with other activities. Having the proper environment and mindset will enable you to accomplish more with the time you have set aside to do this reading.

After you have cracked the cover, preview what you intend to read. Take a minute or two to make an overview of, survey, or skim the pas-sage in its entirety. Read headlines, photo captions and graphics, sub-titles, and the first and last paragraphs. Then ask yourself what you already know about this topic and anticipate what you will learn more about as you read. Finally, write down two or three questions that you hope this reading will answer or address.

This step is very important. Previewing helps us connect the known to the new; it primes the pump of mental association. Rather than jumping in blindly, we get some idea of what to expect, a better sense of the big picture, when we preview. Previewing also fuels our curiosity.

### During: Read, Monitor, and Annotate

The second step to Power Reading occurs in the "during" phase, a complex process wherein we read, monitor, and annotate. Although complex, this process need not be baffling or difficult.

First, read slowly, pausing frequently (at least once per section or page) to gauge your comprehension of what you have just read. This is called self-assessment or self-monitoring, and it is essential to reading well. Saying the words, whether silently or aloud, is merely decoding; it is not real reading in any sense of the word. Power Reading is all about comprehension, so if you didn't grasp what you just decoded, do it again.

Of course, your receptive vocabulary — the words you know when you read or hear them — will play a large part in your ability to comprehend. We understand more and more readily when we know the language or jargon, the words or terms common to the topic or discipline. If you come across a word (or several) you don't know while reading, don't be discouraged. Try to figure it out from the context (sentence or structural clues), and if that doesn't work, circle the word(s) to look up or ask about later. Then carry on.

If you give up reading because the vocabulary is tough, you will always only know or believe what you already know or believe. Systematic vocabulary expansion will improve your reading comprehension. Just don't get hung up on that as a goal every time you begin to read.

When reading in areas or disciplines with which we are least familiar, we need to stop and check our comprehension more often than we do when we're on more familiar ground. For example, I check my comprehension every hundred words or so when I'm reading about physics, but only every two to three hundred words if I'm reading about reading. My master's degree is in the teaching of reading; I have taken only one physics class in my life.

As you read and monitor your comprehension, "talk back" to the text — and its author — with the pencil you have in hand. Mark up the text. Pencils are far better for this type of annotation than highlighters or pens, largely because pencil can be erased.

When you annotate:

- Place asterisks (**) next to main ideas.
- Circle unfamiliar words and write "Def" for "Define" alongside them.

- Place a question mark (?) in the margin next to anything confusing or unclear to you.
- Place an exclamation mark (!) beside anything especially intriguing or important.
- If an idea strikes you as personally relevant, or if you have a personal example to illustrate it, write "Me" or your initials in the margin.
- Write "Dis" for "Disagree" and a brief note as to why when you come across thoughts with which you disagree.
- Ideas with which you strongly agree might merit triple exclamation marks (!!!).

For more suggestions toward improving your annotation abilities, see the section "Note-Taking while Reading" later in this chapter.

### After: Paraphrase, Summarize, and Review

After you have finished reading, monitoring, and annotating, glance quickly over what you have just covered and write down answers to your anticipatory questions. Then select two or three of the most difficult ideas to paraphrase, or restate in your own words. It is best to actually rewrite these passages in language you understand, perhaps in a separate venue such as with your class lecture notes. Next, close the book and write a one- or two-sentence summary of the main idea, as you understand it, in what you have just read. Finally, take a few minutes immediately to review your answers and annotations (marginal notes), along with anything you have paraphrased, and your summary. Review of the material read is most productive when it is both immediate and frequent. Revisit your written response to reading as frequently as you are able, and you will reap the benefits of Power Reading in no time.

## SQ3R (Survey/Question/Read/Recite/Review)

The principles of SQ3R are very similar to those of Power Reading. Each involves action to be taken before, during, and after reading. Each reading strategy also encourages the reader to preview and formulate questions, read for answers, write the answers, and then review. Both Power Reading and SQ3R subscribe to the core principle that meaning is made in a dynamic exchange between the reader and the writer. Both strategies emphasize that meaning-making, or comprehension, is an interactive process with the author, reader, text, and context all playing pivotal roles.

Briefly, the steps of SQ3R are as follows.

### Survey

Take sixty seconds to skim what you are about to read. Look at headlines, boldface type, and graphics — get a sense of the big picture. Read the first and last paragraphs; ask yourself what you already know about this topic.

## Question

Based on your survey, think about what questions this material will likely answer or address. Then write down three or four general questions that you hope to answer by reading this material. Practice turning headings/ titles into questions. For instance, a chapter in your psychology text on bipolar disorder may lead you to ask, "What is Bipolar Disorder?" "What causes it?" "How is it treated?" It is important to write out your questions before you begin reading, as doing so provides both focus and purpose for your reading. It helps you concentrate.

## Read

Look for answers to your questions as you read, and stop to write out those answers as soon as you come to them. Read with a pencil in hand and make marginal notes as needed. Set a goal for yourself in terms of minutes to read or pages to be read, and don't stop completely until you have reached this goal. Make note of difficult concepts you will want to review to clarify and new words you will want to define.

## Recite

After reading, annotating, and writing answers to your questions, read aloud both the questions and answers several times. If you have summarized the main idea or a summary is provided, reread that also, aloud, to cement it in your long-term memory. Recitation is a means of memorization, of transferring information from your short-term to long-term memory. As with building vocabulary, the best way to recite is orally: read, reread, then repeat.

## Review

Take a second look, a third, and then another. The best reviews are frequent and periodic. Research shows that reviewing material immediately after you read or hear it increases retention and reduces study time by more than 75 percent. With SQ3R, before previewing a chapter or assignment, review the previous chapter or assignment. Review your annotation and written questions/answers also; review all main ideas you have memorized via recitation. To review, revisit, recap, repeat, recite, and read are similar acts; each improves retention and recollection. You can recite and review with a study partner, too: Ask each other questions and check the accuracy of your responses.

| TRY IT!   STRATEGIC READING |
| --- |

Use Power Reading or SQ3R with your next textbook reading assignment. Afterward, bring your text to your instructor during office hours to show him or her your annotations, or how you marked it up. Bring also any written questions and responses that your reading generated. Ask the instructor to critique your effort and suggest improvements.

## EXPAND YOUR VOCABULARY

For most of us, our *receptive* vocabulary (the words we understand when we read or hear them) is much larger than our *expressive* vocabulary (the words we actually use when we speak or write). Linguist, wordsmith, and syndicated columnist William Saffire says that a well-educated person has a receptive vocabulary of about 20,000 words but uses only about 2,000 when speaking.

One reason to work at closing this gap and expanding our vocabularies in general is to understand more of what we read and hear. Words let us think about and make sense of the world. Name the world and we own the world.

Another reason for vocabulary development is to express ourselves well and precisely and to be understood. Articulate people get what they want more often than inarticulate people because words give us power within our environment and with other people. Long considered a measure of intelligence, vocabulary expands as we learn and become more knowledgeable. In college, we come to know an academic discipline first through its vocabulary.

To expand your receptive and expressive vocabularies, make an effort on two fronts. First, adopt a systematic approach to gradually increasing your store of words in fields of study that are new to you. While you listen to lectures and read textbooks, circle or write down new words; then follow the suggestions in the "TRY IT!" exercise on page 45.

On the second front in your vocabulary expansion effort, adopt a "Triple A," an Attitude of Attentiveness and Awareness to new language in everyday conversations. Whether in or out of the classroom, this attentiveness will keep you alert to opportunities for informally adding new words to your store. Play language games, such as Scrabble or any of the dozens on the market. If you view language acquisition as enjoyable, it soon becomes exactly that.

**TRY IT!   BUILD YOUR VOCABULARY**

In a small notebook or on 3-by-5 cards used solely for this purpose, define and learn new words by following these steps:

1. Write the word (and its context if possible) on one side of the card/page.
2. Write the dictionary definition on the other side of the card/ page.
3. Ask someone, your instructor or a friend, to define the word for you; then modify or add to the dictionary definition accordingly.
4. Note word origins (etymology) and alternate meanings.
5. Use this word in conversation or in writing at your earliest opportunity.
6. Review periodically.
7. Check your progress now and then by reciting definitions with a partner or friend or as a self-test.

WRITING TO REMEMBER

### Note-Taking While Reading

If you are reading textbook material, have your class/lecture notebook also at hand. In this notebook, write down each reading assignment, date, and all the questions, answers, and summaries you generate to extract main ideas from your reading. Then, as you read, make marginal notes in the text with the following tips on page 46 in mind.

## TIP!  STRATEGIC NOTETAKING

1. Always read with a pencil in hand.
2. Use a system of consistent, personalized symbols to note
   - ideas mentioned in class.
   - material with which you agree or disagree.
   - material with which the instructor agrees or disagrees.
   - ideas that resonate with your prior reading.
   - ideas that contradict your prior reading.
   - anything confusing.
   - controversial claims or issues.
   - ideas you can connect with personal experience.
3. Write down predictions and questions before reading that you expect your reading will prove or answer. Then, while reading, write down answers to these questions.
4. Use Post-It Notes (3-by-5) to mark pages and to expand the space available for note-taking.
5. Underscore or star important passages; annotate the text by writing in the margins. If you are worried about defacing a book, you can always erase pencil. Annotating text while you read allows you to engage the author in a dialogue, which is the epitome of active reading.
6. Keep writing. Don't stop! Note-taking is a habit, a good habit, and one formed as most habits are: with practice.

### Paraphrasing and Summarizing

To paraphrase is to restate or rephrase an idea in your own words; *para* — as in parallel — means "analogous, like." To summarize is to restate an idea in fewer words; a summary captures the gist (the sum/the whole) briefly, economically.

Skillful paraphrasing and summarizing can markedly improve your reading comprehension, and this skill can be had with practice. It is far less effective, though, to think about writing a summary than to actually do it: The written record provides a more efficient means of study than you can get by rereading alone.

Authors of textbooks often include summaries for you, the reader. Again, these are useful but not nearly as useful as writing your own. Whole-chapter summaries may be an ambitious beginning anyway; this sort of comprehensive recap writing is a goal to work toward in steps.

Where best to begin? Begin by underlining the topic sentence or main idea in each paragraph or short section you read. Some paragraphs have no main idea, and the topic sentence is not always the first. As you read and underline, don't puzzle for too long. If the emphasis isn't obvious, skip it and move on.

When finished reading, recopy these underlined sentences sequentially, adding transitional words as needed. Read and reflect on this summary; omit needless repetition. Finally, paraphrase your compilation of main ideas in as few words as possible and write out the paraphrased summary with your class notes.

Another way to practice paraphrasing and writing summaries is to answer who/what/where/when/why/how questions about the assigned reading. Practice abbreviation, too, as a way of capturing essential content in summary form. For instance, "Nature is the term for genetic makeup or biological inheritance" becomes "Nature = genes." Restating ideas in your own words makes them personal and meaningful for you. If this sounds difficult, try the "TRY IT!" exercise that follows and you'll soon be a paraphrasing pro.

---

### TRY IT! PAIR UP TO PARAPHRASE

An excellent way to practice paraphrasing is to ask a friend to select, then read aloud to you, two paragraphs from *Study Skills for College Writers*. Immediately afterward, paraphrase what was read to you. Spend no more than three minutes writing this; then compare your version with the original. Fill in gaps and correct obvious errors. Choosing relevant texts, take turns reading aloud so that your partner might also practice his/her paraphrasing.

---

## REMEMBERING

We can help ourselves remember by "writing it down," but even this will not ensure perfect recall. We forget for nearly as many reasons as we remember; however, I've yet to meet a college student who wanted to better her ability to forget.

Remembering is mostly about intention. If we read and listen with the intent — the desire — to remember, chances are we will. By contrast, we can easily forget without intending to forget. I remember my students' names because I have a desire to do so, not because I have been blessed with extraordinary powers of recall.

## Memory Is Fickle

Along with being driven by our conscious intentions and desires, memory is also influenced, and more subtly, by the subconscious mind. It is selective. Sometimes it protects us from pain by blocking out trauma. We remember the highly unusual, too, more than what is ordinary.

Despite the fickle nature of memory, most of us have little trouble recalling what is genuinely important to us. The harder task, of course, is remembering what does not (yet) seem personally relevant. Students remember and learn readily in, and hence usually get good grades in, subjects in which their interest is already high. How can we sharpen our recollection when interest is not so high? Here are some ways to improve your powers of recall:

- **Write it down.** The best aid to memory is the written reminder. Writing down what you hope to recall — be it the "to do" list or your instructor's "five principles of learning" — frees up thought time for new input and other ideas.

- **Cultivate interest.** Ask and answer the question "Why should I care?" Generating interest is often no more involved than thinking through consequences and connections.

- **Tell someone.** Verbalizing what you hope to remember helps, as does having the person you tell, in turn, remind you.

- **Post reminders.** In places you are sure to see, such as on the bathroom mirror or refrigerator door, post a written reminder.

- **Recite and review.** Nothing beats repetition for active memorization.

- **Give yourself a leg-up.** A leg-up is a boost, as into the saddle on a horse. One leg-up for remembering more is using the memory techniques called *mnemonics*.

## Mnemonics

Mnemonics works on two principles: the mental process of association and the idea that the smallest unit of communication is the symbol. A wink, a stoplight, the Golden Arches, a letter of the alphabet — all are symbols and all evoke associated responses.

Logos are symbols with widespread recognition, often worldwide. Think again of those Golden Arches or the hood ornament on a Mercedes Benz. These symbols are a type of mnemonic meant to trigger all sorts of associations. While logos can be fun to design, other mnemonics are somewhat simpler. Common ones include:

- **Abbreviations and acronyms** (a word formed from the first letters and syllables of other words). NSF is an abbreviation for National Science Foundation, while NASA is an acronym for National Aeronautics and Space Administration. HOMES is an acronym for the Great Lakes; MI is an abbreviation for Michigan.

- **Reconfigured acronyms.** Sometimes an important series of letters is difficult to recall precisely because it cannot be pronounced or does not make implicit sense. When this happens, you can invent your own associations, reconfigure or flesh out the symbol or command. For instance, a friend was having trouble remembering "http://," so he invented this mnemonic: "Home To The Paddock: Whip Whip."

- **Pseudonyms, codes, and passwords.** If you want to personalize impersonal information, it often helps to create a code, a pseudonym (alias, pet name), or a password that has special significance for you. Ideally, this word (or combination of symbols) then triggers a chain of associated responses.

- **Rhythm and rhyme.** Put new words to an old tune you know by heart, or write a rap/melody for a text you are trying to memorize. We remember what has rhythm and rhymes exceptionally well; just think of all those song lyrics you could sing in your sleep.

- **Visuals.** Convert abstract ideas into concrete mental pictures. For example, the following are simple graphic symbols for abstract, complex concepts: ♀ ♂ $ ☯ ⚖

The principle here is that, at its root, communication is symbolic. A graphic or pictorial representation can call forth a whole host of associations at a glance.

---

**TRY IT!   CREATE YOUR OWN MNEMONIC**

Invent your own mnemonic for a list of items or a complex concept you want to commit to memory, preferably for an upcoming test. Write or draw it here; then share your invention with a friend. Ask your friend to quiz you with this mnemonic just before your test.

---

## TO REVIEW

Your reading comprehension and retention will improve as you become strategic, apply Power Reading methods, and work to expand your vocabulary and heighten your general attentiveness to language in all its written forms. Read actively by writing in response: annotating, paraphrasing, and summarizing. Taken together, these practices will strengthen memory, as will your intent to remember.

# — Chapter 6 —
# Listening and Note-Taking

Listening is the first and best language act and language art. As toddlers, before we speak, read, or write, we listen — and by listening we learn. In the hierarchy of language acquisition, to listen holds primacy; it is our most essential, elemental mode of learning. Unfortunately, many of us unlearn to listen as we grow older; we find we prefer talking instead — after all, we have so much to say! Also, our growing facility with other language acts sometimes gets in the way, and we realize that listening well (again) demands attention. It takes some work. Fortunately, a few gentle reminders are often all we need to jump-start an early command of this most essential communication skill.

This chapter addressed active listening — the only kind that counts — in the context of the college classroom. In classes, listening is frequently tied to note-taking, or it should be. Notes are a product of our studies, a record we create together with a speaker, and they can make or break our success in certain spheres. Note-taking, I am happy to say, is a skill we can readily improve with practice. This chapter offers many tips for taking superb notes and for using those notes to maximum advantage.

## LISTEN UP!

In the fifth edition of *The Art of Public Speaking*, author Stephen E. Lucas claims that "close to 90 percent of class time in U.S. colleges and universities is spent listening to discussions and lectures. A number of studies have shown a strong correlation between listening and academic success. Students with the highest grades are usually those with listening and academic success. Students with the highest grades are usually those with the strongest listening skills."[2]

Most of us know intuitively that listening well is linked to successful communication of all kinds — in the classroom, at the workplace, and at home. We may know, too, that we can be better listeners but are unsure of how to do so. Because listening actively is vital to learning, it makes sense to begin by identifying causes of poor listening behavior. Next, we'll examine steps we can take to become stronger, more active listeners. Finally, we'll consider the academic (and other) benefits of comprehensive listening, and we'll look at the link between effective listening and effective note-taking.

[2]Stephen E. Lucas, *The Art of Public Speaking* (New York: McGraw-Hill, Inc., 1995), p. 51.

## Interference, or Inactive Listening

Many factors interfere with our ability to listen well. These include:

1. Having difficulty concentrating.
2. Drawing hasty conclusions.
3. Listening too critically.
4. Focusing attention inappropriately.

Concentration requires us to block out an endless barrage of external and internal distractions, which may range from a growling stomach to the sunshine outside to the cute guy sitting on your left. By far the most frequent distraction, though, is the noise in our heads, the constant stream of thoughts that may or may not have to do with the spoken message to which we are trying to attend. Our brains can process about three times as many words per minute as can be spoken; this leaves a great deal of thought time while listening, during which our thoughts can wander.

A second contributor to inactive listening involves drawing hasty conclusions. We do this when we think we know what a speaker is going to say before he or she says it, so we tune out the speaker, or basically stop listening. Often our hasty conclusions are wrong, as are the assumptions we've made that led to them. This behavior is not only inactive listening; it is anti-learning, antithetical to the learning process. When we put words into a speaker's mouth we are communicating poorly — frequently with the very people to whom we feel closest, our families and friends.

Another way in which we sometimes dismiss a speaker prematurely is to prejudge his or her message as boring, ill-informed, or misguided. Active listeners suspend judgment, hold their tongues, and hear out a speaker fully before drawing conclusions.

Similar to judging hastily, it is also possible to be too critical of a speaker. If we focus solely on the flaws in his or her speech, we may miss much — if not all — of what is useful, right, or true. We listen better, remember more, and are able to apply it when we extend to speakers our goodwill, the benefit of the doubt, the same respect we would hope to be given were our roles reversed. To learn from listening requires that we respect speakers and expect to learn.

One last common cause of interference with effective listening is focusing attention inappropriately. Instead of attending to the message, to what is being said, we focus too much on how it is being said (delivery) and this interferes with optimal comprehension or understanding. If the speaker clears her throat in a manner that annoys you, you might find it extremely difficult to focus on what she is saying. Along with getting caught up to our detriment in matters of presentation (the *how*), we also sometimes focus inappropriately on the speaker's appearance or manner. While these visual, nonverbal clues can aid communication, sometimes they are needless distractions that thwart active listening.

### Listening Actively: A How-To Guide

Improvement begins with self-assessment. Once aware of our challenges as listeners, we can take steps to become better listeners. The first step is to recognize that listening and hearing are not synonyms; listening is voluntary, whereas hearing is involuntary. We have no choice about much of what we hear and overhear (traffic, the rain, the radio in the room next door), but we have enormous choice about what we listen to or to what we attend. Active listening means we choose to listen, intending to understand and remember. It requires concentration, thought, and reflection.

The next step is to minimize distractions, both physical and mental. If you are thirsty, get a drink; then return to listening. Make a note to say hi to that cute guy after class; then return to listening. Tell yourself, "Yep, that's one ugly tie my instructor is wearing today"; then return to listening. When our attention wanders (as it will now and then), we can make a real effort to rejoin any speaker's message by anticipating what will come next or reviewing what she/he has just said. Write it down. Taking thorough notes is a time-tested way to listen actively, resist distraction, and sharpen our ability to stay focused.

Another step toward active listening is to suspend judgment and avoid assessing harshly or attending only to flaws. Finally, we can remind ourselves often that the package (or presentation or delivery) is never as important as its substance. What a speaker says matters more than how she/he says it — almost every time.

---

### TRY IT!   HOW WELL DO YOU LISTEN?

Hone your active listening skills by evaluating your current listening practices. Describe, briefly, your strengths and weaknesses as a listener. List two situations in which — or two speakers to whom — you don't. Explain what makes the first effective and the second ineffective. Identify three things that the ineffective speakers could do to better deliver their messages and three things that you, the listener, can do to better comprehend and recall what is said.

## *College Success and Comprehensive Listening*

We listen for varied purposes: to appreciate, to empathize, to be entertained. In college, much — perhaps most — of our listening is for the purpose of learning. Comprehensive listening, or listening for understanding, is thus the type of listening that students most frequently seek to improve.

Comprehensive listening is active listening; it requires participation on the part of the listener. Just as we cannot be passive readers, we cannot be passive listeners — both processes demand the involvement of at least two communicators. Comprehensive listening is the kind we do in classrooms during lecture and in small or whole-group discussion. Our skill with this language act depends heavily on prerequisite skills with memory, concentration, and vocabulary.

In the fourth edition of *Listening*, authors Wolvin and Coakley write,

"The effective comprehensive listener . . .
  • has a strong desire for memory improvement, concentrates on memory improvement and practices memory improvement
  • develops self-discipline to control distractions, is self-motivated to listen, and accepts responsibility for the success of each communication interaction in which he or she is a participant
  • strives continually toward vocabulary improvement."[3]

Active, effective, and comprehensive listening is a big part of college success, and vocabulary, concentration, and recall are integral to comprehensive listening. Moreover, the benefits of comprehensive listening extend beyond the classroom into all areas of our lives, all our relationships as communicators. Successful students, favored employees, and cherished mates and friends routinely cite "skillful listening" as a key attribute of earning said distinction.

For specific suggestions on how to improve your vocabulary and remember more of what you read and hear, see Chapter 5. For specific suggestions on how to improve your concentration while listening, check out the tip on the following page.

[3]Carolyn Gwynn Coakley and Andrew Wovin, *Listening*, 4th ed (Dubuque, Iowa: Wm. C. Brown Publishers, 1992), p. 222.

## TIP! CONCENTRATING CAPABLY

Concentration begins when we tell ourselves to pay attention and take note, when we intend to remember. Follow these tips if you want to excel at listening:

- In the classroom, we can concentrate more easily if we sit up front, sit up straight, and minimize distractions.

- No amount of good intentions can compensate for lack of preparation, though, so get to class early and review the reading assignment; also review your notes from the last class meeting.

- Anticipate the day's lecture by checking the syllabus and reflecting on your prior knowledge of the topic. Link the known to the new. Perhaps write down a question or two you believe the speaker may answer or at least address.

- To be at our most mentally alert and able to concentrate, it is essential that we be rested, well fed, and in good health.

- Finally, to stay focused, start writing — taking notes — as soon as the speaker starts speaking. As you do, listen for verbal cues that alert you to important points or ideas, such as "the thing to remember here is . . ." If (or when) your attention begins to wander, don't berate yourself for the lapse. Concentration, like memory, isn't perfect, and we all have occasional lapses. Instead, find the speaker's eyes and follow them, locking into eye contact until you have come back, fully, to what she/he is saying.

## TRY IT! HOW WELL DO YOU CONCENTRATE?

Keep a running log of your concentration behaviors for one meeting of the class for which you are having the most trouble listening/paying attention. In the left-hand column of your notes, place a checkmark whenever you find you have stopped listening, or whenever you catch yourself "tuning out." Place a star in your notes when you find you are listening intently. Immediately after class, review this record. Are patterns discernible? What behaviors of the instructor or your classmates trigger an attentive or inattentive response from you? In one or two sentences, record the conclusions you draw from this self-monitoring effort.

## NOTE-TAKING

Good listening abilities are closely linked to good note-taking abilities; being adept at the one enhances the other. Your notes are a text you create together with a speaker, but there's a twist: Unlike textbooks, your notes are highly personal, and they are frequently more relevant and memorable than text material because of your active involvement in their creation. Good note-takers, like good students, are made, not born. Good notes, however, are born of active listening.

### *Your Notes*

Why do we take notes? We take notes to learn, to understand, to guard against forgetting. We take notes to have a record from which to study and prepare for tests. We take notes to free up brain space for new ideas and information.

Over the years, many students have told me that they come to college having had little or no note-taking experience. College classes are often larger than high school classes, and lecture is a more frequent mode of instruction in college than in high school. These two factors combine to render many (maybe most) first-time college students inexperienced note-takers, so if you feel like a novice in this capacity, you're in good company.

Experience can be had, of course, by trial and error; however, this may not be the best path. Your notes will be an asset without parallel in your quest for academic success if you are thoughtful and diligent in their making.

What characterizes good notes?

- Good notes are complete but concise, thorough but not belabored.
- They are clear and coherent; they recap and communicate the instructor's key points.
- They also contain your thoughts, questions, and reactions to the address or lecture.
- They are legible, useful, and often revisited.

What characterizes good note-taking? Although it may seem contradictory, two traits that describe this practice are being flexible and consistent. An effective note-taker is flexible enough to do so in different ways for different purposes yet consistent in that she/he takes notes habitually, regularly, as a matter of course. Whether note-taking from lecture, discussion, or reading, you, too, can be flexible, consistent, and effective by minimizing distractions, developing a note-taking system (or systems), and believing that this skill has salient, genuine academic benefits.

## Minimizing Distractions

Learning what tends to distract you in the classroom and what you are able to ignore or overcome is one possible outcome of the "TRY IT!" exercise on page 54, your running log of concentration. Maybe you are more often led off-topic by internal than external distractions; for instance, you can block out the chattering of your classmates but not your worries about money. Whatever the distraction, disarm it by seeing it as a distraction, not a legitimate recipient of your attention at the moment.

Tell yourself that your only legitimate concern right now is this speaker and this class; practice being present in the present, an active listener, note-taker, and college student occupied with learning and not preoccupied with past or future matters. You can't do anything about that busted muffler while here in class anyway, so focus on what you can do; engage with the topic and the people at hand. Imagine that this is your job and you are being evaluated on how well you do it. Because you have invested in yourself, paid tuition for the opportunity to be in this class, you have a financial interest, too, in making the most of your time and efforts.

To inhabit the present fully, to be occupied and not preoccupied is easier said than done. Still, we know what it feels like when we are so totally engrossed in what captures our attention that a freight train could pass within a few feet and we'd scarcely notice. Being enraptured — or even entertained — may be a tall order for the classroom to fulfill; however, investing our energy in staying engaged is well within our reach.

## Developing a Note-Taking System

A good system or two for taking notes is indispensable. By *system* I mean a planned procedure, a semi-structured approach. Adopting a systematic approach, or method, for note-taking helps us get started and have an idea how to continue. Methodical note-taking also fosters efficient review or study because this approach tends to produce more orderly, organized, and coherent notes than does note-taking in a haphazard, nonsystematic fashion.

A few note-taking systems popular among college students are:

- the Cornell System (and its variations: columns and key words [*split screen*], fact versus idea, cause/effect, compare/contrast)
- informal outlining
- mapping
- précis

Good note-takers use some variation of these systems without necessarily knowing the name. Each system can be adopted and adapted to suit your personal needs, whether you take notes on paper or with a hand-held or laptop computer. Let's look a little more closely at the defining features of each system (see Appendixes 2–6 for examples of each system).

### The Cornell System

The Cornell System makes use of two columns: a right-hand record column for recording main ideas, concepts, facts, and examples, and a left-hand recall column (perhaps a two-inch-wide margin) where notes to the right are summarized or called to mind with key words and phrases. The recall column should be completed as soon after the lecture as possible. This system can help you study by offering a built-in, self-test feature: Cover the record column and try to recall the information it contains by using the key words and phrases in the recall column as prompts.

There are variations of the Cornell System for note-taking that also use columns and key words. Your paper (or screen) can be split in half to record principles (main ideas) on the right and facts or examples (supporting data) on the left. If the lecture is organized by cause/effect or to compare/contrast two entities, this split-screen method also makes good sense. Use a variation such as this for taking notes only if you are able to discern the pattern of organization the speaker, your instructor, is using.

### The Informal Outline

Perhaps the method college students use most frequently to take notes is the informal outline. In this, indentation and numbers serve to group information categorically, keeping ideas of equal importance visually separated from ideas of lesser, or subordinate, importance. Done well, this produces orderly, tidy notes; however, it requires an ability to grasp emphasis — or relative importance of data — very quickly on first hearing. If the speaker's material is organized and presented as such, outlining can be a great system. Conversely, it can be futile, frustrating, and produce inferior notes if the speaker's presentation is disorganized.

### The Mapping Method

The mapping method of note-taking is particularly apt for visual learners. To "map" your notes, locate the main idea or lecture topic in the center, at the hub. Then, as significant details are presented, write them along lines (or spokes) that connect to the main idea they support. This method functions well with lectures that seem disorganized, or if the inherent structure is not immediately clear.

### The Précis System

The précis system is perhaps the most difficult, most sophisticated way of taking notes discussed here. A précis is a summary or a synopsis, and skill with paraphrasing and summarizing is required for using this system to best advantage. With this approach, after listening for a few minutes and mentally processing input, the note-taker intermittently records brief summaries or short paragraphs of what she/he has heard. Advantages include having put the material into your own words, thus personalizing it for ease of recollection. Disadvantages include the difficulty factor and the chance you'll miss important information while composing summaries as you listen.

---

## TRY IT!   PRACTICE A NOTE-TAKING SYSTEM

Experiment with a method of note-taking new to you. Using the Cornell, split-screen, informal outline, mapping, or précis system as described, take thorough notes for the duration of a class conducted largely by lecture. Afterward, reflect on the experience and the quality of these notes. What worked? What didn't? Review these notes just prior to the *next* meeting of this class. Again, listen attentively and take notes as you do. If the system you used before worked well, use it again. If not, try another. Swap your notes with a classmate to compare, contrast, and discuss.

---

Becoming a better note-taker takes practice. Here are some suggestions you might try when note-taking from a lecture:

1. **Sit front and center.** From here you can see the board, hear the instructor, and make eye contact.
2. **Date notes and number pages.** Put name, phone number, and "reward for return" on the front and back cover of your binder/ folder. Notes sometimes do get lost; they are more likely to come back to you if a reward is offered.
3. **Keep notes separate for separate classes.**
4. **Write legibly.**
5. **Use a system to distinguish points of emphasis, more or less important ideas, main ideas, and supporting data.**
6. **Use standard and personalized abbreviations** (e.g., B = Bartleby; char dev = character development).
7. **More is generally better than less.** If unsure as to importance, write it down. You can always condense or omit, but "adding" after the fact is difficult.
8. **Write down even the obvious.** It may seem obvious today, but you'll have forgotten what "it" was three weeks down the road.
9. **Reread each day's notes.** Try to do it quickly, before leaving the lecture hall. Add to anything that needs clarifying; flesh out half-formed thoughts; fill in gaps.

10. **Write a one-sentence summary of each lecture's main idea.** Summarizing is a very good way to wrap up notes.

11. **When reading and studying from your notes, get involved.** Highlight your notes or retype them; read aloud. Shuffle notes up, read them out of order, and then resequence them properly.

12. **Compare your notes with a classmate's; ask the instructor to review.** Both of these acts require courage but can be very rewarding.

Your notes are a text YOU create and will be as useful as you are committed. Imagine that you are being paid for the quality of the notes you take: Are you earning top dollar? Work toward the priceless.

---

**TRY IT! TEST YOUR NOTE-TAKING SKILL**

For a class in which you are concerned about the quality of your notes, seek a second opinion. Swap notes with a classmate, and then get together to discuss their similarities and differences. Visit your instructor during his/her office hours with your notes in hand and a few specific questions about what you have written and how she/he thinks you might best study from or improve these notes. An open mind and the willingness to experiment will bring results.

---

IN SUM

The benefits of effective note-taking are many. Good notes promote efficient study and test preparation. They enhance listening and reading comprehension and retention. Reinforcing one another, active listening and note-taking are essential skills for college success.

# — Chapter 7—
# Problem-Solving

Problems! From the moment we wake until our heads hit the pillows again, we face — and face down — problems, make decisions, resolve conflicts. Critical thinking and problem-solving (or decision-making) go hand in hand; they are, in some ways, three different names for the same process.

The ability to effectively solve problems and resolve conflicts is a characteristic of good students, favored employees, and team leaders. As we develop this ability, we must first establish the need for resolution, sometimes examine causes, and carefully consider approaches, alternatives, and possible outcomes. Thinking both "inside" and "outside" the box, both critically AND creatively, will ensure that innovative, fresh ideas rise to the top.

Making decisions and resolving conflicts is a fact of adult life. As adults, college students face more choices than ever before. Some find this freedom exhilarating, some find it overwhelming, and some find it both in approximately equal measure.

With the privileges of college life come the responsibilities. Students must make an ever-increasing number of decisions about academic matters and, perhaps even more so, about interpersonal relationships. Most of us have no trouble making simple daily decisions, such as wheat or rye, socks or not. It is the harder choices that perplex us — those that are thorny, complex, and problematic: Which section of which class should I take and when? How can I live with this person who likes this crazy music? This is when we need a trusted approach or an advisor, some guidance and a little direction with problem-solving.

## EFFECTIVE ACADEMIC PROBLEM-SOLVING

Academic problem-solving involves decisions we must make about our schooling, or studies, such as how to manage time, apply for a scholarship, find a major or minor. These practical problems can be simple or complex; they do not, however, usually involve a conflict we are having with another person.

Academic problem-solving may also refer to the problems we are asked to consider, and often must propose solutions for, within our course of study — from math to music, economics to ecology. These "academic" problems (e.g., What's the best way to lower inflation?) are often sizable in scope, affecting large numbers of people.

Interpersonal problems differ from academic ones in that they directly involve a conflict we are having with another person. Interpersonal problems may, of course, adversely affect our studies, but they do not arise immediately from those studies. Academic and interpersonal problems are more alike than they are different, but for ease of discussion I've divided them into two camps here.

### Gather Information, Evaluate

When the decisions to be made or the problems to be solved are academic in nature, we are wise to begin by gathering information. This information might concern issue identification, the need for resolution, the status quo, possible causes, possible outcomes, and options or alternatives for response. We might be expected go further still by examining implications of a suggested solution or questions arising from implementation. Ideally, information-gathering is a nonjudgmental step that leads us to make informed decisions or draw educated conclusions.

Gathering and evaluating information is a crucial critical-thinking skill — so crucial that we've devoted a chapter to it in this book. Here, let's apply it to two common concerns of college students.

Pick topic A or B below, and then answer questions following in detail:

A. **Class selection.** This is a practical decision students must make again and again.

B. **Paying for school.** For you, this year, this may be a hypothetical problem. In the future, however, it may again be of more immediate concern.

1. **What type of information will be most useful?** (e.g., for topic A: course catalog, time schedule, a calendar, published student evaluations of instructors)

2. **Where is this information and how do I obtain it?** (e.g., for topic A: check the school Web site; call or visit the registration office)

3. **Is this information valid and reliable? How do I know?**

4. **What other, secondary sources of information might help me with this decision?** (e.g., for topic A: teachers, other students, academic advisors)

5. **What are my two top priorities (objectives) with respect to this decision?**

6. **Does the information I've gathered help me meet those objectives?**

## TRY IT!  ACADEMIC PROBLEM-SOLVING

Now think through an academic issue or decision currently
concerning you and answer the preceding questions 1 through 6.

### *Professor Quiel's Problem-Solving Paradigm[4]*

When speaking or writing at length about a problem that affects large
numbers of people, a systematic approach to proposing a solution will
be most persuasive. Building a case to advocate your solution is a form
of argument, and formal argument derives its power to persuade, to a
great extent, from its form. Is it logical? clear? coherent? complete? One
paradigm — or blueprint — for persuasively exploring problems and proposing solutions looks like this:

- creative, attention-getting introduction
- introduction to problem area
  - specific statement of problem
  - thesis/proposal
    - need: scope (how big?)
      - intensity (how bad?)
    - cause(s): immediate and ultimate
    - failure of the status quo
  - support: it works/can work
    - evidence
    - desirability/feasibility
- implementation

Let's say you want to propose a solution to the very real problem of
school violence. As you write your speech or essay on this topic, flesh
out each of the items in the skeletal schemata above. Tell your audience
why you care, what the problem is, and how many it affects and how
badly. Be sure to illustrate why current "solutions" are not working and
why you believe yours will. Use evidence (facts/examples/statistics) to
support all claims, and close with a word about how your proposed
solution should be enacted. When solutions are proposed in this careful, formal way, they tend to move an audience to act.

In the June 18, 2001, issue of *Time* magazine, an article by Jeffrey
Kluger details a new approach to curbing binge drinking on college campuses that is having remarkable — and somewhat unexpected — success.

[4]Laurie Walker, "Courting Persuasive Prowness" English Journal, 79 (December 1990):
87.

Organized according to the problem/solution paradigm just outlined, this article finds that when student surveys self-reporting the frequency of alcohol consumption are publicized around campus, binge drinking drops. This campaign of information — correcting misinformation — has been far more effective than other, earlier efforts. Binge drinking a problem? Reduce the problem by demonstrating that it isn't as widespread as rumor would have it.

### Seek Expert Assistance

Sometimes even our best efforts at solving academic problems are ineffective. They end in uncertainty or get bogged down by competing claims. We see advantages AND disadvantages or fear that the solution may do more harm than good. When this happens, when we are in doubt, it is time to seek help. Again, the most effective help will come from those qualified to give it — those who have experience with the kind of issue or problem we are trying to resolve. For extensive discussion of help-seeking, turn to Chapter 2. After reviewing these guidelines, relax. Make the call. Ask.

---

## TRY IT!  ACTIVE PROBLEM-SOLVING

Think about a decision or conflict you are currently grappling with that concerns — or has come up in — one of your classes, perhaps as a topic for further discussion. Describe the problem, briefly, in writing. Then describe the best solution you can imagine and one or two acceptable, alternative outcomes. If appropriate, plug your problem (say, violence in schools) into the paradigm outlined above and think it through accordingly. Next, list three or four sources of information you could use to defend or reject this proposed solution or decision. Gather information from at least two of the four sources. Finally, before you take action to effect your decision or solution, run the plan by a trusted advisor. Ask him/her for a recommendation and any other feedback he/she feels comfortable offering.

---

EFFECTIVE INTERPERSONAL PROBLEM-SOLVING

### Whose Problem? Issue Identification and Ownership

Conflicts that involve other people can make our lives miserable, and needlessly so. Most conflicts of this sort begin as minor annoyances or misunderstandings; then they snowball into major matters that are impossible to ignore. Your roommate leaves his clothes in a pile at the foot of the bed. It bothers you, but you say nothing; it's his bed and they're his clothes, after all.

Soon, a second pile starts — on your side of the room! Your irritation gives way to anger, and now you can't study with those clothes in your presence. Days later, fed up, you finally see your roommate when you and he are both awake. "You're such a slob," you say. "Can't you at least keep your dirty clothes in your own half of the room?" By way of response, he shrugs; then he moves the second pile in front of the door — the only door — on his way out that door.

This problem is your problem. You own it. If it bothers you more than it bothers the other party, you have primary responsibility for seeing it resolved. It may seem unfair that the person "at fault" does not assume this responsibility, but if acceptable resolution is truly your goal, you must assume it, take charge.

First, identify the issue or problem as clearly as you can. To do this, use "I" language rather than "you" language (see the "TRY IT!" exercise on page 66). "I" language focuses on our own needs, desires, and feelings rather than on those of the other person(s). It tends to diminish defensiveness, whereas "you" language fuels it. "You" language sounds accusatory. For example, "You are such a slob" is a putdown and assigns fault. Conversely, to say, "I do my best work in a setting that is clean and orderly," gets the point across in a clear, honest way and is less likely to generate resentment. Using "I" language is an assertive approach to conflict resolution; it is neither passive nor aggressive.

After articulating the conflict to your own satisfaction, owning it, you are ready to informally negotiate resolution. It is possible to do this if both parties are willing to talk.

### Negotiation Considerations

Most interpersonal problems can be solved at the negotiation stage. Conversation is a powerful healer and should be given its due. Negotiation requires good listening skills and a bit of time. It is preferable to mediation, and when it works, both parties involved in the resolution feel better for it. Here are some tips for effective negotiation:

- **Make a date.** Agree on a place and time to talk where you won't be disturbed. Try to make it a neutral place if possible.
- **Talk in turns.** Avoid interrupting when it isn't your turn. Allow the other person to finish his/her thought before you respond.
- **Express your concerns candidly, honestly.** Use "I" language.
- **Sustain eye contact.** This is very important.
- **Address specific behaviors rather than beliefs.** Focus on what the other person *does*, not who he/she *is*. Nine times out of ten, action is

what we need to acceptably resolve conflicts, so zero in on the offending action and the desired action.

- **Listen carefully.** Make a sincere attempt to understand the other
  person's position and concerns. And resist the urge to explain or
  justify your behavior in response to what you hear.
- **Seek clarification in your attempt to understand.** Repeat what you
  think the other person has said (e.g., "So you're saying . . .").
- **Brainstorm possible solutions together.** Good idea!
- **Compromise.** Avoid either/or thinking, as in either your solution or
  mine. Promises made under duress are seldom kept. Only when both
  parties feel somewhat satisfied is a solution likely to work. Consider
  lots of alternatives; be creative, be willing to give up a little to get a
  better return.
- **Take the first step by offering a concession** (e.g., "I won't have
  guests in the room after 11 on weeknights") and be prepared to coun-
  teroffer and consider new options.
- **Keep your promises.** Abide by all agreements. Be sure that what you
  agree to is clear, doable, and understood. Vague agreements are pretty
  much useless, so be specific. Spell out precisely who must take what
  action.

## *Mediation Considerations*

When negotiation fails — as it occasionally will — mediation is the next
step. This involves bringing in a third party, preferably an objective, neutral party, if those in conflict are no longer speaking and emotions are
trumping reason. Mediation is really mediated negotiation, with the
mediator acting as referee to ensure civility and an opportunity for both
parties to be heard. Mediation can be binding (as are judges' rulings),
but it doesn't have to be. Parties in conflict generally determine the outcome themselves.

Because of their experience, trained mediators are the most effective.
They are also often difficult to find when you most need one. Many
colleges and universities, however, have groups of student mediators
(sometimes an offshoot of student government) who will serve to arbi-
trate peer conflicts. Again, it is smart to determine the availability of this
service well before the heat of the moment when you need to make use
of it.

Why is negotiation preferable to mediation? First, it enables you to
work on communication and conflict-resolution skills so that you can
avoid needing mediation in the future. Second, it is easier to live with
the consequences of your own decisions and agreements than with those
imposed on you by others. Nobody likes to feel strong-armed or co-
erced. Given the choice, most of us would prefer to act of our own free
will.

---

**TRY IT!   DEFEAT DEFENSIVENESS: "I" VERSUS "YOU"**

Consider a current problem you are having with another's behavior — behavior that is adversely affecting you. What would you like to say to that person in an effort to end the offending behavior? In a few short sentences, write that message here:

_____

_____

_____

_____

Now look again at what you have written. Do your sentences open with "you" or with "I"? Is the tone descriptive or accusatory? Do you find fault or do you state feelings? Next, rewrite your message in "I" language. Try to banish the pronoun "you" entirely. For instance, "You never clean the bathroom" is better expressed, "This bathroom needs cleaning. Can I get some help?" If you have a hard time with this, begin by completing these incomplete sentences:

I feel _____ about _____ because _____

I think _____

I want _____

I need _____

I hope _____

When interpersonal conflict resolution is the goal, "I" language invariably works better than "you" language.

---

### Win/Win Resolution

Effective conflict resolution avoids the either/or fallacy (e.g., either right or wrong, yes or no, your way or my way). When two or more people have differences and hope to reach an agreement that each party can live with, this generally requires a compromise or an alternate solution that neither party has yet considered. In a compromise, agreement is reached through mutual concession. Each party gives a little, meets in the middle, and settles. Alternate solutions usually come about when both parties brainstorm together, neither sticking stubbornly to his/her first thought.

A good compromise does not produce winners and losers. It occurs if the parties involved see themselves as collaborators trying to solve a problem rather than as adversaries or opponents. If you are able to solve a problem or reach an agreement to mutual satisfaction and mutual gain, you have achieved a win/win resolution.

## THINKING CRITICALLY AND CREATIVELY

Critical thinking is the way in which we make sense of the world, adapt, evolve, and plan for change. It requires basic problem-solving skills, such as identifying the problem, brainstorming, evaluating options, and choosing and enacting the best possible option. There is more to thinking critically and creatively, however.

Along with logic and intuition, induction and deduction, truly innovative thinking uses an experimental mindset. The experimental mind has the following qualities:

- It questions ceaselessly, challenges assumptions, rejects conventional wisdom, and is seldom satisfied with "the way things are."
- It looks from many angles, forestalls judgment, and gathers information.
- It solicits opinions, brainstorms freely, and can sustain the paradox of seeming contradiction.
- It considers alternatives, is curious and concerned, and works within a safe environment.
- It is open and receptive.

Creative and critical thinkers have always challenged the status quo. Susan B. Anthony didn't just give up when told she couldn't vote; Martin Luther King Jr. went to jail rather than "accept" the status quo. The Wright brothers, Henry Ford, Thomas Edison — all heard their fair share of "it can't be done" before their inventions revolutionized our lives. For a critical and creative thinker, satisfaction comes with positive change, and with the sharing of the benefits of discovery with others.

### No Problems, No Progress

I can't imagine a world without conflict; nor do I think I would want to. Conflict is not all woe and misery; some is enormously beneficial. Without it, our lives would be uneventful, static, and bland. A state of conflict is prerequisite if change is to occur; if we always think what we've always thought, we will always do what we've always done.

Discovery, invention, and innovation are the products of conflict. It is inherent in sports, science, government, free enterprise, and every other competitive venture. Conflict is necessary if democracy is to thrive; witness the U.S. Supreme Court, with its majority and dissenting opinions.

To some degree, attitude matters where conflict is concerned. Do you see the cup half empty or half full? Are problems simply problems, or are they challenges, too? In "The Stunt Pilot," a treatise on beauty, discovery, and learning, Annie Dillard says, "Nothing on earth is more gladdening than knowing we must roll up our sleeves and move back the boundaries of the humanly possible once more."[5] Without problems, there can be no progress.

---

### TRY IT!  CHALLENGING ASSUMPTIONS

Test your mental acuity by taking this brief quiz (the answers follow). You may need to "think sideways" or reconsider your initial assumptions to see these questions/answers from this point of view.

1. How many birthdays does the average person have?
2. Some months have thirty days, some have thirty-one. How many months have twenty-eight days?
3. What is tomorrow if today is the first day of the week?
4. I have in my hand two coins that total thirty cents. One is not a nickel. What are the coins?
5. Divide thirty by one-half and add ten. What number do you get?
6. It is illegal for a man to marry his widow's sister. True or false?

Answers

1. one
2. twelve
3. Monday
4. a quarter and a nickel
5. seventy
6. true (he's dead)

---

[5]Annie Dillard, "The Stunt Pilot" from *The Best American Essays*, College Edition, 3rd ed, (Boston: Houghton Mifflin Co., 2001), p. 138.

**TRY IT!  THINKING OUTSIDE THE BOX**

A frequent assumption among college students is that it costs money to have fun (e.g., "Anything fun is expensive, illegal, or unhealthy"). Below, list nine fun things to do that defy these assumptions.

1.                     2.                     3.

4.                     5.                     6.

7.                     8.                     9.

## TO REVIEW

It would be great if we could solve all of our problems simply by wishing it so. However, because wishful thinking works only occasionally, a more methodical approach to problem-solving boasts a better success rate. If the issue or decision you face is academic, begin by articulating the problem precisely and establishing the need for resolution. Next, examine causes, effects, and tried and untried solutions; gather and evaluate pertinent information; examine alternatives; and seek a second — or third — opinion.

If the conflict or problem is interpersonal, identify and own it; then follow the guidelines offered for effective negotiation. Practice using "I" rather than "you" language and work toward win/win resolution whenever possible. Finally, the more adept we become at thinking critically and creatively, the easier problems are to solve. Exercise your mind: Imagine.

# — Chapter 8 —
# Test-Taking

Taking tests need not be an anxiety-filled experience. If you're prepared — overprepared — attend class faithfully, and practice sound testing principles, you, too, can test with the best and show what you know. Tests are a favored means of measuring what we have learned and what we can do. Tests demonstrate competence and capability and give us useful feedback. We take tests to pass classes, gain admittance to programs of study, land jobs, and obtain certification to practice trades and professions. Regardless of the purpose for any particular test, systematic attention to the process — preparation, completion, and review — will produce desirable results. Read on and listen up, and soon, if you are not already, you will be testing like a pro.

## PREPARATION, COMPLETION, AND REVIEW

### *Preparation*

The best way to prepare for a test is little by little, day by day. It is easier, less stressful, and more productive to study for tests in this incremental, methodical fashion than to cram.

Cramming may be better than not studying at all, but not much better. It increases anxiety and decreases stamina, the energy your brain needs to function at its best. If you have been studying little by little, day by day, the time you might otherwise spend cramming would be better spent getting an extra hour of sleep. To most successfully prepare for a test, attend class faithfully, take notes, review your notes, and read all of the assigned material. Reread whenever possible.

For effective study strategies and to have the right tools and materials to prepare for tests, review the information-gathering, listening, note-taking, and power-reading suggestions provided in Chapters 4, 5, and 6. Then, about one week before your test, do the following:

- **Anticipate the type of test you will take.** If the instructor hasn't specified, ask. The larger the class, the more likely the testing will be "objective" — multiple choice, matching, true/false. You can determine with some accuracy the type of tests you will likely take before you enroll in any given class. To do this, check class capacity. If you would rather take essay tests than objective tests, for instance, enroll in a small class.

- **Inquire about study guides, tutoring, or review sessions for the exam.** If available, take advantage of these opportunities. Some instructors keep "old test files" and are more than willing to share these sample questions with students. Student organizations also often keep old test files; it may be worth your while to ask if such files exist.

- **Clarify what remains unclear in your understanding of your notes and assigned reading.** If this means paying a visit to your instructor during office hours, do it! If you can fill in the gaps by studying with a friend or fellow classmate, do it. Check your understanding of course content with a peer, first by swapping notes and then in conversation.

- **If you have no idea what to expect on the first exam in a class, think about the course so far and your prior experience with similar courses.** Have the lectures been mostly informative (objective test), or have they involved considerable interpretation (essay test)? If you have spent more time in class discussion than in lecture, expect essay tests. Also, the number of questions about a topic, on a well-written test, is typically in proportion to the time spent on that topic in class.

- **Ask your examiner what to expect.** How long will the test take? What will it ask? How much is it weighted toward the final grade? How does she/he recommend you study for this test? Ask, too, what you may (and should) bring to class on test day: A bluebook? A calculator? A dictionary? A watch? Your book? Pens? Pencils? Then make sure you have everything you need at hand.

- **On the night before the test, turn in early and sleep well.** Eat healthy (not heavy) food about one hour before your test. Walk briskly for a spell, if you can, to get blood flowing to your brain, and always dress comfortably when taking a test.

---

### TRY IT!   CREATE A STUDY SCHEDULE

Working backward from your exam date, construct a three- or four-day study schedule. Write down specific hours and specific tasks. Consider inviting a classmate or two to join you for one or two of these sessions. Be sure to set — and meet — a reasonable goal for each session.

---

## TRY IT!   PREPARE AHEAD

Especially if you have only a fuzzy idea what your examiner will ask, make up your own test questions, based on a reasonable assessment of course content. Look over your reading and notes and then write down several possible questions. Answer these questions fully. Ask a classmate to do likewise; then swap your questions. Compare your answers, too. Show your sample test question(s) to your instructor and solicit his/her response.

---

### *Completion*

You have your test in hand and are ready to roll. Take care to stop, at this point, and complete the two most important items: Put your name on the test and read all directions carefully. Listen closely, also, to any announcements about or amendments to the test. Then look over the whole test once before you dig in. If there are varied point values for varied sections, budget your time accordingly. Do a rough calculation of how much time you have to answer each question. Start by answering the questions for which you feel best prepared; this will build confidence, increase your overall score, and may yield "clues" to questions you are less sure about. Have a system for marking or denoting questions to which you will return; for an essay or short-answer test, also note in what order you will answer these questions.

As you read, be sure you understand what the question is asking. If unclear, mark that question and continue. When you have finished the rest of the test, raise your hand or approach your instructor; ask him or her for clarification. Instructors want you to do well. Most are more than happy to clarify or paraphrase a question if they can. Take care not to overread or overinterpret test questions, too. If a question seems simple or easy, that just means you know the answer! Instructors who intentionally try to "trick" students are very, very rare; most have an investment in being well-regarded and fair.

When should you guess on a test? First, when you know there is no penalty for doing so and, second, when you have no better basis for making a choice. If, however, you must guess, guess wisely.

## TRY IT!   TEST STRATEGY: MULTIPLE CHOICE

When reading multiple-choice questions, anticipate the answer. Look for it among the options. If you don't see it or something similar, proceed by eliminating obviously wrong answers. Then consider what's left. If more than one remaining option seems correct, choose the one that best answers the question or completes the sentence. Look for the familiar, for ideas that were often repeated in class, for the most inclusive option. Bear in mind that the easiest type of statement for an examiner to write is one he/she believes to be true.

## TIP!   "NONE OF THE ABOVE"

Because it is difficult enough to write one plausible foil (wrong response) let alone four or five, "none of the above" is seldom the correct test choice. "All of the above," however, because of its inclusiveness, is more commonly correct.

## TRY IT!   TEST STRATEGY: ESSAYS

Before you begin an essay test, jot down a skeletal outline, your central claim and two or three supporting examples or points you most want to include. This will guide you as you write and show the examiner evidence of your planning and forethought. Once writing, open with the question rephrased as a statement. Don't bother with a lengthy introduction; your instructor knows what he or she asked. Keep these testing strategies in mind:

- Support all claims with examples — excerpts from the text, lecture, or discussion.
- Be concise and neat. Your ideas matter most, but presentation counts, too.
- Use transitions, "sign posts" (first, next, then) to promote ease of reading.
- Use everyday language; write as you would speak. Prefer the simple and straightforward to the complex and convoluted.
- Leave blank space after each response and write on every other line.
- Ask if a bluebook is appropriate.
- Be as reader-friendly as you can. Remember, the person reading this exam will be reading many in a short time. Anything you can do to be clear, coherent, and concise (yet complete) will be appreciated.
- Use all of the time allotted.
- If allowed, bring and use a dictionary.
- Leave yourself a few minutes to proofread for spelling, grammar, and punctuation.

Again, if you have questions or need clarification while writing an essay test, approach your instructor and ask. Other tips for writing winning essay exams appear later in this chapter.

## TIP!  USE *ALL* OF YOUR TIME

During a test, whether it is an objective or essay format, use all of the time available for its completion. Students often feel such relief as they close in on the last line of a test that, in their eagerness to be done and gone, they sabotage their chances for the best possible grade. Take a deep breath and spend a few minutes reviewing what you have done. When you are satisfied that this represents your best effort, turn in the test.

### *Review*

Once you have completed a test and have truly given it your best, reward yourself in some appropriate small but significant way. Phone an old friend you haven't talked with in a while or make a date with a new friend to workout; share a meal with someone. While it is better to save big-time celebration for big-time accomplishment, even routine accomplishments — such as tests — deserve recognition.

When your graded test is returned to you, review it carefully. Make note of the questions for which you were best — and least — prepared. Is there a pattern here to either your difficulty or success? Which types of questions did you answer well or poorly? Which of your study and test-taking strategies worked and which didn't? How might you modify your approach to studying for the next test in this class (or of this type) based on your performance on this test? Determine why "right" answers were right and why others missed the mark. Then learn from your mistakes: Take time to outline better responses.

If, after careful review, you remain uncertain as to how the test was scored, make an appointment to review it together with your instructor in his/her office. This will speak volumes of your commitment to the class and to your education in general. Such conversations can also give you much useful test-taking advice and help clarify the subject matter. Instructors typically enjoy talking with their students one to one, especially talking about what they teach, their areas of expertise. Test reviews create a very real opportunity for this to happen; however, nine times out of ten, the student must initiate the conversation.

Students occasionally take tests in college that are not returned to them unless they approach the instructor or assistant and request to review the test. This happens most frequently in large lecture classes, where scores for objective tests are posted. Test review is valuable; it is your responsibility and your right. Always ask to see your test after it has been graded.

## TRY IT! HOW WELL DID YOU DO?

After your first test in your most difficult class, whether you
scored as highly as you had hoped or not, write down five things
you intend to do differently as you prepare for your next test,
based on your findings from this first test review. Then make your
intentions come true. Do at least four of the five. After the second
test, assess the success of your modified preparations.

### OBJECTIVE VERSUS SUBJECTIVE TESTS

Objective tests can include questions of the true/false, matching, multiple-choice, and fill-in-the-blank variety. Answers to these questions have been "predetermined" (i.e., there is only one right answer), so anyone scoring the test (often a machine) will come up with the same score. This is unlike essay — or subjective — tests, where the person scoring makes a "subjective" judgment about the quality of the response. Objective test responses are either wholly correct or incorrect; subjective test responses can be correct or incorrect in part.

### *Objective Tests*

When taking objective tests, keep the following strategies in mind:

- If half a statement is true and half is false, the whole statement is false. (In other words, a little poison poisons the well completely.)

- Words such as *always* or *never* are absolutes that tend to render statements untrue. Conversely, words such as *seldom* or *often* are qualifiers, which tend to render statements true.

- The one word most likely to change a true statement to a false one (or vice versa) is the word *not*.

- Multiple-choice and matching questions are much like "multiple" true/false questions: Each option is either correct or incorrect and can be considered a separate question in turn.

- Objective tests require you to use your time wisely, to carefully read all directions and questions and consider all alternatives.

- Avoid overinterpreting questions.

- Don't be afraid to change answers; first hunches are not always right.

- Have a system for reviewing responses.

- Ask for clarification when necessary.
- Use all of the time allotted.

---

### TIP!   IS YOUR TEST WELL CONSTRUCTED?

Occasionally an objective test is poorly constructed. When this happens, the correct answer may be

- longer than the incorrect answer(s)
- qualified to give it precision
- not the first or last in the series
- not one of two similar (or opposing) options
- not a joke or an insult
- not in unfamiliar language or technical terms

These are clues of last resort. Most objective tests are well-constructed. When you have better reason to select an answer, use your reason.

---

### Subjective Tests

When taking essay tests, keep the following strategies in mind:

- Read all directions and questions carefully, plan your time, and then begin with the questions for which you feel best prepared.
- Jot down a skeletal outline, two or three points you intend to include.
- Organize your answer.
- Open with the question rephrased as a statement. For example, "What caused the War of 1812?" becomes "Causes of the War of 1812 include . . . " Avoid lengthy introductions. Get to the point immediately.
- Use relevant facts, examples, and text excerpts to support your answer.
- Include only one main idea per paragraph.
- Use transitions to unite or separate ideas and provide your reader with direction, some notion of "where this is headed."
- Write to an uniformed reader. Do not assume reader familiarity.
- Conclude with a brief summary of your main point(s).

- Take time to proofread your response. Be as reader-friendly as possible. Spelling, grammar, punctuation, and legibility are all important. Make your presentation clean and clear. Ask your instructor if she/he has preferences concerning how you format your essay test.

### Criteria for Grading Essay Tests

Here are some things that instructors look for when grading essay tests:

- Fidelity to the question. Did the student understand and address it completely?
- Central claims that are well-reasoned, well-supported.
- Responses that are orderly, clear, coherent, and comprehensive but concise.
- Fresh thought, new ideas.
- Writing that is clean, clear, engaging, and easy to decipher. Polished presentation and "neatness" earn students higher grades on essay exams than they earn for the same exams in sloppy, hard-to-read form. Instructors will regard your response favorably at a glance if it appears that you have taken the trouble to consider their needs.

## TRY IT! CONVERT QUESTIONS INTO STATEMENTS

Practice converting essay test questions into statements with which to begin your response. Use questions from tests you have already taken and write out your "opening" statements. Do three or more; then rephrase each statement and write it "in other words" without altering the meaning. If you have no essay tests on which to practice this, take a crack at converting the following:

- Identify the sin of which the Big Bad Wolf is most guilty in the story "The Three Little Pigs."
- Why do birds fall in love? Explain.
- List three positive outcomes of the civil rights movement in America that Martin Luther King Jr. helped lead.

### Essay Test Verbs

The verbs in essay test questions are key because they tell you what to do, how to craft your response. For instance, *discuss* differs from *define*, which differs from *compare* or *criticize*. Being asked to *trace* Hamlet's development as a character requires an entirely different response from the directive to *evaluate* it on psychological grounds or *contrast* it with Ophelia's. Attend carefully to the verbs used in essay test questions. If you are unsure as to what they are asking you to do, consult your instructor for clarification or confirmation.

---

**TRY IT!  TESTING VERBS**

List at least eight of these kinds of verbs — directives or action words — that you might conceivably see on an upcoming test in a current class. Swap your list with a classmate; then draft sample essay test questions for this class using at least three of your listed verbs.

---

**TIP!  TESTING ANXIETY**

Anxiety about taking tests is normal. Some anxiety is helpful (it gets our brains moving and says that we care), but too much anxiety is anything but helpful. The best way to combat test anxiety is to be overprepared; occasionally, though, adequate preparation alone does not erase our fears. If you find yourself anxious before a test, plan to arrive early and get a good seat in front where you are less likely to be distracted by others. Don't sit by friends and avoid chatting with classmates before the test; use the extra time for quiet review. Survey the whole test before you begin. Read instructions carefully and plan how you will proceed. If you start feeling anxious during the test, stop. Put down your pencil/pen, cover your eyes, breathe slowly and deeply, and then stretch a bit to get comfortable. When you feel calmer and more focused, pick up the pen/pencil again. Skip questions that stump you and return to them later; ask to have the question paraphrased or clarified if need be. Use all of the time allotted. Be thorough with proofreading or response review. And remember: A moderate adrenaline surge can improve your performance on tests. The goal here should not be to eliminate test anxiety but to keep it channeled or contained. Above all else, think positive thoughts. You can do this!

## IN SUM

Once again, tests show what we know and what we can do. While not the only means with which to demonstrate competence, tests remain one popular method, particularly in schools. Prepare for your next test by reviewing the principles and practices described throughout *Study Skills for College Writers,* and may you find yourself, post-test, with reason to celebrate.

# — Chapter 9 —
# Strategic Study and Collaborative Study

Strategic study is an approach to learning and an attitude. Students who strategize undertake their studies with plans of action. In other words, they know where they want to go and how best to get there, and they are seldom deterred for long by the inevitable obstacle. To study strategically is to study with a purpose. It begins with the goal clearly spelled out, often in writing. As an approach, strategic study builds confidence; it fosters a "conceive it/believe it/achieve it" attitude. Best of all, strategic study affords peace of mind. It eliminates the need for cramming, frees up time, and lightens the load. Strategic study prepares us to perform beyond our potential.

Collaborative study is yet another way to lighten the load, via the time-honored tradition of teamwork. Frequently, two heads or more are better than one: When we work together we accomplish more, and more quickly, than when we work alone. Collaborative study enables us to fill in the gaps, check errors, share the workload, and be social all at the same time. Group learning promotes cooperation, clear communication, responsibility, and accountability. Collaboration is everywhere in the larger world of work. When we study and work together, we learn from our peers.

## STRATEGIC STUDY SYNTHESIZED

Strategies for successful study are presented throughout *Study Skills for College Writers*. These include ways to improve your goal-setting, help-seeking, reading, writing, note-taking, test-taking, time-management, problem-solving, and decision-making abilities. In this chapter we'll synthesize these ideas and suggest a comprehensive, strategic plan or approach that, if enacted, will help you study smarter, not harder, and enjoy your college experience for the unprecedented opportunity it can be.

### *A Strategic Approach to Learning*

Several principles that govern all learning also support the strategic approach to study discussed throughout this book. I first encountered these principles while co-authoring the college success text *Right from the Start* (now in its third edition), with Dr. Robert Holkeboer. Dr. Bob says that we "retain information and learn most effectively"[6] when we

1. Have a genuine interest in the subject.
2. Define subjects in terms of real experience and concrete problems.
3. Write and speak about the subject under study.
4. Work with others.
5. Reward our learning.
6. Connect the known to the new.
7. Establish personal purposes for learning.

To transform these seven principles into a concrete, strategic plan of action, let's begin by enacting principles 1, 2, 4, 6, and 7 in the "TRY IT!" exercise that follows.

[6]Robert Holkeboer and Laurie Walker, *Right from the Start: Taking Charge of Your College Success*, 3rd ed, (Belmont, CA: Wadsworth Publishing, 1999), p. 18–21.

## TRY IT!   INTEREST/EXPERIENCE INVENTORY

What subjects interest you? How might your past experiences help shape your course of college study and eventually your career? Ask your roommate or a new friend to do this short interest/experience inventory with you. Take turns interviewing each other with the following questions and record responses. Completing this inventory in this way has a dual benefit: You will learn more about yourself — your potential paths of study and preferences — as well as about your roommate or new friend.

1. What were three of your favorite things to do as a child? What did you do with friends? What did you do alone?
2. What were your two favorite subjects in high school? Were you involved in extracurricular activities? Which? Which were the most satisfying?
3. List three of your talents — things you do better than most people do.
4. List any hobbies or vocational pursuits.
5. Name your two most significant accomplishments to date.
6. Have you traveled somewhere that you especially enjoyed? Where? Where on the planet would you most like to visit? List your top three destination choices.
7. What do you read? What kind of movies do you enjoy?
8. What recreational activities do you do alone? with friends?
9. What is your dream job? Describe it.
10. What classes and what activities here on campus interest you most just now?
11. Where have you worked? Briefly recap employment history.
12. Name three people you admire. Why do you admire them?

After you and your partner have completed this inventory, study your list and then your partner's to see what patterns you might perceive. Based on the responses, can you predict areas of study in which you (or your partner) are likely to excel? What are they? Write down three or four.

### The Strategy of Self-Direction

All seven of the principles of learning I have just noted can be put to work for you with self-direction. Akin to motivation and goal-setting, self-direction basically means telling yourself what to do, and then doing it. Good students and able learners are highly self-directed; they know what they want and go after it with purpose and a plan.

Here is a simple, three-step strategic planning approach to self-direction.

## Step 1. Assess your situation.

As with problem-solving, we begin here by taking stock, gathering information, and asking questions.

## Step 2. Define your goals and objectives.

Keep your goals briefly stated, realistic but challenging. Use upbeat, positive, specific language rather than downbeat, negative, and vague language when spelling out your goals. For instance, "Earn an A in algebra" is more specific language than "Do better in math."

## Step 3. Establish timelines, accountability, and indicators of success.

Break your goal up into smaller steps and schedule a reasonable amount of time to complete each step. Also, determine before you begin how and to whom you will demonstrate your commitment to this cause and how you will measure or gauge incremental and ultimate accomplishment. In other words, how will you know when you've achieved your goal? How will you let others know?

If you find your enthusiasm for school waning now and then, remind yourself of your personal purposes for seeking higher education. Spell them out, post them, revisit them in a letter to a friend, but articulate in some way *why* you choose to be in college. Connect your interests and prior experience (the known) to what you are learning (the new). Write and speak about it; share with others. Finally, when your planning pays off and you do achieve an objective, reward yourself! My mother likes to say, "I catch more flies with honey than vinegar," and the same is true of self-direction: We respond better when we reward rather than deprive or punish ourselves.

Dr. Gary Evans, a motivational speaker at Eastern Michigan University, tells a great story about self-direction. It goes like this:

A ten-year-old boy came into the lunchroom carrying his lunchbox. He sat down and, as he had the day before and for as long as anyone could remember, he opened the box, sighed, then said, "Peanut butter again." One day a classmate, a girl sitting nearby asked the boy, after his sigh, "Who makes your sandwiches?" The boy replied, "I do."

So who makes *your* sandwiches?

## TRY IT!   CONNECT THE KNOWN TO THE NEW

The ultimate goal of strategic study is to improve learning. Practice by connecting the known to the new and the new to the known to move yourself closer to this goal. Set a timer for five minutes and, during that time, write down rapidly all you can think of to say in response to this prompt: What are the characteristics of good writing? In other words, what do you look for in a piece of writing to capture and sustain your interest? When five minutes have elapsed, review what you have written, what you "know" about good writing. File this with your English composition class materials or text. As you learn more or other characteristics of good writing, revisit and add to or modify this list; connect the new to the known.

## COLLABORATIVE STUDY

Collaboration exists everywhere in the world of work. Cars are designed and manufactured in teams; television shows are written in teams; major motion pictures require the work of vast numbers of people. Throughout business, industry, and government, collaborative decisions and projects are the order of the day; even artists, sole proprietors, and entrepreneurs need patrons, employees, and investors.

While there may be times when each of us works alone, autonomously, we eventually come together with others to do our best work. Increasingly, employers expect employees to be capable collaborators.

In college, in part to prepare for and mirror the demand for it in the work-a-day world, group work is a frequent occurrence. Whether we form groups ourselves or they are formed for us, we come together for many varied reasons. Groups meet needs.

Humans, as we've said, are inherently social. Along with the all-encompassing notion that we need one another to survive, we put our heads together to solve specific problems and complete specific tasks more efficiently and effectively than we could if acting alone. We gather to enjoy the company of others, learn from one another, share common interests and pursue common goals.

Collaborative study is a form of group work that promotes cognition, cooperation, interpersonal communication, and leadership skills. Because we value or respect the opinions of others we perceive to be "like us," we learn from our peers more permanently and more often than we do from authorities or experts. When we work with them, our peers hold us accountable for our words and deeds. We are responsible for both our own actions and those of the team.

## Ground Rules for Collaborating

Teams formed for purposes of study or academic project completion function best if a few simple ground rules or guidelines are observed:

1. Come prepared. Bring relevant — and supplemental — materials. Plan to stay for the duration of the agreed-on time.

2. Whenever possible, keep groups stable or intact for a period of time. Stable groups tend to cohere and productively work out their disputes. They capitalize on individual strengths once those strengths become apparent.

3. Collaborate in groups of four to seven members. Smaller groups have insufficient resources and larger groups can be chaotic. Report out or join with a larger group (such as the whole class) after achieving the initial objective in the smaller group.

4. Volunteer or elect, and then rotate, the following for each group session: a facilitator, a recorder, a timekeeper, and a devil's advocate (see the definitions near the end of this chapter). Taking turns fulfilling these roles is important, especially if the group is to cohere over time.

5. Clarify the objectives (goals or agenda) for each team meeting or session at the beginning; then review what is accomplished at the end. Establish tentative objectives for the next group meeting before you disband.

6. Respect your collaborators' opinions and ideas and expect their respect in return.

7. Listen first before you respond. Keep comments constructive and avoid evaluation — unless you are the designated devil's advocate!

8. Avoid dominating the discussion. Give all members equal airtime. Encourage the involvement of reluctant participants by asking questions, inviting their opinions.

9. Stay on task. If the group gets sidetracked, be a leader and bring your team back to task.

Meeting with a small group to review assigned reading or materials presented in class is a great way to reinforce learning and to prepare for tests. Research supports collaborative study; students who study together average higher test scores than do students who study alone.

## TRY IT!   THE "A" TEAM

Take the initiative to form a study group for a class for which you believe it could be helpful. Invite three classmates to join you once a week for an hour at a mutually acceptable time and place. If one or two decline your invitation, keep asking others until you have at least four committed team members.

Meeting an hour just before or after class often works well, and the student union, dining commons, library, or a lounge near your classroom or instructor's office are perhaps better meeting places than the residence halls.

Keep the group small but stable with four to five members, and meet in the same place at the same time each week. Exchange phone numbers and e-mail addresses at your first meeting.

Before you begin, copy, distribute, and read together the guidelines for productive group study or teamwork provided here. Also, agree from the outset that your priorities are academic. Social camaraderie is a secondary benefit, but the primary benefit should clearly be enhanced learning and higher grades. As the initiator, be prepared, persistent, and punctual, and the others will follow your lead. For obvious reasons, call yourselves "the A team."

## TRY IT!   CHECK YOUR TEAM'S WORK

Once you have established a study team as described, take turns visiting your instructor during his/her office hours with questions that your team generates. Report instructor response back to the group; then write down new questions and select a recorder/reporter for the following week.

---

## TRY IT!　REWARD YOUR WORK

All this teamwork and cooperation sounds good in theory, you say, but you like competition and find it a powerful motivator. Many do. If true for you — and your team members are willing — pitch a couple dollars each into a pool to reward the group member with the highest score on the next test. Create a second pool for the person whose score improves most from one test to the next, and if your *entire* team average continues to climb, splurge and reward yourselves with a social outing at the semester's end.

---

## TIP!　ROLES TO ROTATE FOR TOP-FLIGHT TEAMWORK

- The **facilitator** gets discussion started, promotes the agenda, and keeps the group on task.
- The **recorder** takes notes to reflect and summarize the discussion; he/she writes down questions and responses and seeks clarification when needed.
- The **timekeeper** calculates how much time the team can devote to each objective at each meeting; he/she attends to the time and works with the facilitator to keep the group on task.
- The **devil's advocate** (for lack of a better term) deliberately adopts an opposing point of view, questions conventional wisdom and simplistic responses, and encourages team members to consider alternate outcomes. He/she frequently says, "What if . . . ," "Yes, but . . . ," and "On the other hand . . ." The devil's advocate keeps the group from reaching agreement too hastily. This team member is the chief "questioner."

---

IN SUM

Two routes to more efficient and enjoyable study are strategic planning and collaboration. The foundation for strategic study is an acquaintance with principles that govern learning and self-direction. To collaborate, or labor collectively, is the means by which most of the world's work gets done. Collaborative study increases productivity and enhances learning as it prepares college students for careers and professions.

# — Chapter 10 —
# The Payoff: Your Reward

What is the definition of a student? One who studies. The habits of mind and behavior we have come to call "good study skills" will serve us admirably throughout college and beyond. Whether in school or out of school, we are students of life; learning is a journey, a lifelong endeavor.

Good habits are as easy to form as bad ones. Each takes shape through emulation, repetition, and reinforcement. So what's the payoff? Obviously, good grades are one payoff. Grades, however, are perhaps only the most immediate reward. Better health and lower levels of stress also follow from smart choices and sound study habits. Sound study habits help to keep us at peak performance mentally, but sound health habits supply the physical and emotional foundation.

The ultimate reward for acquiring — and practicing — good study skills is confidence that you can succeed at every task you tackle. With success comes pride, favor, and privilege. And success breeds success.

You make it happen!

## QUALITY OF LIFE

A college education correlates positively with many factors that influence quality of life. College graduates have higher average lifetime earnings, and they report greater satisfaction with their lives than do non–college grads. We all want to be happy and healthy, fulfilled with our work and the choices we have made. We are more apt to report being happy, healthy, and fulfilled, however, if we have successfully obtained a college degree than if we have not.

Strong, solid study habits and strategies enable academic success. Academic success, in turn, can enable your career in the working world beyond college and prosperity. Now that you have read nearly all of this brief guide to academic achievement, it's time to put down the book, enact the advice, and make the achievement your own. Every day is another, a fresh start, a whole new opportunity to study smarter, not harder.

### Start Smart

Have you ever wondered where the quip "give it that old college try" comes from? I have. And I have a theory to explain it — unsubstantiated, but plausible nonetheless. For most of us, college is a time in our lives when we try new things — lots of new things. We meet new people, visit new places, and entertain new ideas at a rate more rapid than ever before, and possibly ever after. We must, however, be willing to *try* these new things and to learn in the attempt or we forfeit all benefit and discovery. Hence "give it that old college try" entered our lexicon as a way of referring to this spirit of adventure, this willingness to engage and explore.

So you've read the book. What is there to try? Try the "TRY IT!" exercises. Try out the tips and steps and strategies, too. Start smart by being honest in your self-assessment of your strengths and challenges as a student. Stay smart by clarifying your short- and long-term goals, planning how you will move toward those goals and sticking with your plans.

Continue studying smarter by taking stock of your resources, questioning and help-seeking, and gathering and evaluating information. Attention to reading, writing, listening, and note-taking skills will help you learn and remember more of what you read and hear. Practice sound time-management, problem-solving, and test-taking strategies and create opportunities for collaborative study as often as you can. If you do these things, there *will* be a payoff. The rich reward you will realize is that of your own academic success.

## TRY IT!  KEEP A JOURNAL

Many, many changes rock your world. Keep a journal for the first six weeks of school, particularly if this is your first semester at a new school. Whether at your computer or with a pencil and paper, write down and file all of your hopes, dreams, and fears. Record your observations, impressions, and obsessions. You are the audience, so anything goes. If journal-keeping proves a useful repository for ideas, keep it up beyond the initial six weeks. At the semester's end, reread what you have written. What have you learned? How have you changed?

### Be Well and Prosper

Smart studying helps us to stay healthy and decrease our level of stress. It reduces anxiety and boosts confidence; it contributes to a general sense of well-being. When we feel prepared for the daily demands of school and work, we are physically, mentally, and emotionally better able to perform. A sound mind in a sound body doesn't happen by accident, however.

While in college, we can easily get run down and become susceptible to sickness of every sort. We want to do everything and be everywhere — all the time. A perceived "time crunch" and the many expectations we have of ourselves makes it tempting to ignore or postpone physical fitness, yet to do so can spell disaster.

We all have physiological and emotional needs that must be met before we are able to learn. According to psychologist Abraham Maslow, these include the need for food, water, sleep, shelter, safety, and acceptance. If these needs are not adequately met, learning becomes extremely difficult. It takes a back seat, in other words, to more elemental concerns. In Maslow's hierarchy of need, the human need to learn is of the highest order. That means once we have fulfilled the lower-order, physiological needs, we are free to focus on the higher-order needs, such as self-actualizing or reaching our potential. Humans, both as individuals and as a species, have an amazing capacity to learn. But this capacity rests squarely on a foundation of good health.

So just as strategies for effective study help you enjoy better health, strategies for staying healthy will help you achieve academically. It is a win/win cycle, with you as the prime beneficiary. Let's briefly consider some smart choices you can make to be well and prosper.

## Sleep

Experts say young adults need seven to nine hours of sleep per night to function at their best; sadly, most college students do not get nearly this much. Be selfish about your sleep. Make your needs and concerns known to roommates, housemates, and friends. Take naps and avoid stimulants such as caffeine or nicotine. Always get adequate sleep before big events, like class presentations and tests.

## Food

It's fuel. It's necessary for survival. Food can cause problems, however, especially in college, when dorm food and fast food and fear of weight gain often take an unhealthy toll. The key is to eat sensibly, even on the run. Carry fruit and whole-grain snacks; drink juice and water. Avoid pure sugar and high-fat foods, which ultimately sap more energy than they create. If you often feel fatigued, your diet may be partly to blame. If you are having trouble coming up with a sensible eating plan, consult your college directory for a counselor or group who can help.

## Drugs

Medication is best left to the professionals. Nonetheless, college students seem perennially inclined to experiment, and year after year alcohol — the legal drug — leads the list of those most frequently and fatally abused. Alcohol is a depressant, not a stimulant, and it is an exceedingly addictive substance, as is nicotine. While the dangers of smoking have been well publicized in the recent past, the dangers of alcohol have received much less public scrutiny. Still, the statistics are startling. Every year hundreds of American college students die from alcohol poisoning, binge drinking, and driving while intoxicated. To improve both the quality and the length of your life, be wary with this "legal" drug. And steer clear of "illegal" drugs altogether.

## Physical Fitness

Regular, sustained exercise goes a long way toward ensuring a healthy mind in a healthy body and alleviating stress. Also, there are so many different ways to get, and stay, physically fit that we should never feel the effort is a chore. Simply walking between classes or other on-campus destinations is a new opportunity to exercise for many college students. Consider your interests and preferences when determining your fitness goals and how you will achieve them. If you like athletic competition, consider court sports or martial arts. If you like being social but not necessarily competitive, try aerobics. Opportunities to exercise by yourself abound on a college campus: walk, run, swim, skate, cycle, lift weights. Take up archery, golf, or tennis; take a class. It is never too late to learn or to begin a fitness regime.

---

### TRY IT!  GET HEALTHY

List six opportunities for physical exercise that are available on your campus, then rank each in order of personal preference. Make a date (with yourself or a friend) to spend at least thirty minutes engaged with your first choice on this list . . . tomorrow! Next, list the three best places to "eat smart" on campus. Make a similar meal date for one of these three — again, with yourself or a friend.

---

## So Long, Stress

Some stress is good. It gets adrenaline flowing and keeps us awake, alert. Too much stress, however, is downright debilitating. Fortunately, there is much we can do to reduce stress in our lives. Here are just a few effective antidotes:

- **Take a break**
  A brief respite can help you return refreshed to the task at hand. Be sure to leave yourself hints about how and where to restart.

- **Get organized**
  Nothing beats a sense of order for feeling on top of your game.

- **Do something nice for someone else**
  Altruism releases endorphins, a chemical in the brain proven to reduce stress and induce feelings of well-being.

- **Say no**
  None of us is superhuman. When the requests and demands pile up, prioritize — then say yes, or no.

- **Exercise**
  Physical activity is a sure cure for stress. Whether moderate or aerobic, exercise is almost always wise.

- **Wait**
  Sometimes problems work themselves out without your active involvement. Avoid acting rashly; give difficult decisions, in particular, a little time.

- **Do it now**
  This may seem to contradict the previous suggestion, but procrastination is a premier stress producer. To alleviate stress associated with unfinished business, tackle it now.

- **Reward yourself for work accomplished**
  Having fun is an excellent stress reducer, especially when you have earned it.

- **Talk about it**
  If you are having problems, find a friend, a mentor, or a counselor who will listen without making judgments. The act of verbalizing often helps us to better understand our troubles and take appropriate action.

- **Seek help**
  When anxiety or stress becomes severe and persists, go to a trusted mentor, your resident advisor, or the college health services counselor for a referral, or an ear.

## EXPECT YOUR BEST

Confidence builds with every success experienced. Success, in turn, requires that we expect to succeed. When we set the bar too low, our success will ring hollow; we are more apt to fulfill our potential and achieve our capabilities when we aim a little higher than our last, best effort.

As consumers, we purchase goods and services with every expectation that those goods and services will be of high quality. We have high expectations of our professors and peers; surely the standards we set for ourselves should be as high. Having high standards and expectations sometimes means we're our own worst critics, but isn't that better than having our work critiqued more harshly, first, by others?

Naturally, there will be times in your college career when choices or circumstances dictate that a project, paper, or performance be delivered with full knowledge that it is less than your best. If this is the exception rather than the rule, however, you have the right attitude. Nothing succeeds like success. Expect your best.

Employers expect college graduates to have a superior skill set:

- Effective written and oral communication skills
- Creativity and problem-solving skills
- Organizational skills
- Leadership skills

These skills are precisely those emphasized in general education or core curriculum classes, the liberal arts heart of most bachelor's degree programs. Courses in the arts and humanities and sciences and social sciences can strengthen this skill set and make you attractive to employers. While in college, you can also improve these skills outside of class via involvement in co-curricular activities. Finally, your efforts at self-improvement — such as reading this book — should pay off in all of the ways described.

## ENSURE SUCCESS

With superior study skills, college can be more fun, more gratifying, and more life changing than you may even now imagine. A college degree correlates closely with self-reports of satisfaction in life; it generally provides favorable financial and psychic returns.

But you have to want it. Ensure your success in college by driving it with your desire; hold on to your spirit of adventure and exploration — every day. A. Bartlett Giamatti, former commissioner of Major League Baseball and past president of Yale University, entered college with the dream of a dual career in baseball and literature. Overcoming obstacles, he succeeded splendidly. In his address to the freshman class at Yale in 1983, Giamatti had this to say:

> Each of you will experience your education uniquely — charting and ordering and dwelling in the land of your own intellect and sensibility, discovering powers you had only dreamed of and mysteries you had not imagined and reaches you had not thought that thought could reach. There will be pain and some considerable loneliness at times, and not all the terrain will be green and refreshing. There will be awesome wastes and depths as well as heights. The adventure of discovery is, however, thrilling because you will sharpen and focus your powers of analysis, of creativity, of rationality, of feeling — of thinking with your whole being.[7]

[7]From "A Free and Ordered Space." Reprinted with permission in *The College Success Reader*, by Thomas Hoeksema and Robert Holkeboer, Boston: Houghton Mifflin, 1998, p. 57.

Thank you for reading this. In doing so, I hope you have found some ideas to help you achieve your twin goals of classroom and college success. My highest hope, however, is that when you look back ten and twenty years from now you remember your college experience as fondly as I remember mine.

# — Appendix 1 —
# Weekly Schedule for a Full-time Student (Five Classes) Working Twenty Hours per Week

| 7:00 AM | Monday | Tuesday | Wednesday | Thursday | Friday | Saturday | Sunday |
|---|---|---|---|---|---|---|---|
| 8:00 | Wake, shower, etc. | Wake, shower, etc. | Wake, shower, etc. | Wake, shower, etc. | Wake, shower, etc. | Wake, shower, etc. | Wake, shower, etc. |
| 9:00 | Eat, etc. | Eat, etc. | Eat, etc. | Eat, etc. | Eat, etc. | Eat, etc. | Eat, etc. |
| 10:00 | English | Study Math | English | Study Math | English | Work | Church |
| 11:00 | Speech | Math ↓ | Speech | Math ↓ | Speech | Work | Church |
| Noon | Study History | ↓ 12:30 | Study History | ↓ 12:30 | Study History | Work | Family |
| 1:00 PM | History | Eat, read | History | Eat, read | History | Work | Family |
| 2:00 | Work | Study | Work | Study | Work | Errands | Family |
| 3:00 | Work | Telecom | Work | Telecom | Work | Wash clothes | Family |
| 4:00 | Work | ↓ 4:30 rest | Work | ↓ 4:30 rest | Work | Shopping | Study |
| 5:00 | Work | ↓ Rest | Work | ↓ Rest | Work | Cleaning, etc. | Study |
| 6:00 | Swim | Swim | Swim | Swim | Swim | Swim | Study |
| 7:00 | Eat, etc. | Eat, etc. | Eat, etc. | Eat, etc. | Eat, etc. | Eat, etc. | Eat, etc. |
| 8:00 | Study | Study | Study | Study | Study | Study | Plan for week ahead |
| 9:00 | Team mtg. | Study | Team mtg. | Study | Socialize | Socialize | Plan for week ahead |
| 10:00 | Sleep | Study | Sleep | Study | Socialize | Socialize | Sleep |

# — Appendix 2 —
# Note-Taking:
# The Cornell System

The Cornell system uses two columns: The right-hand column is for recording main ideas, concepts, facts, and examples, and the left-hand column is where the right-hand notes are called to mind with key words and phrases.

*Psychology*

*Mon., Jan. 1*

*4 p.m.*

| | |
|---|---|
| *mental health* | *The three major mental illnesses are: (1) schizophrenia, (2) bipolar disorder, (3) depression* |
| *(psychosis)* | *A break from reality; often masked by hallucination or delusional thinking* |
| *schizophrenia* | *Psychotic reactions characterized by withdrawal from reality with highly variable accompanying behavioral and intellectual disturbances* |
| *bipolar disorder* | *Sometimes called manic-depression, this disorder is characterized by dramatic mood swings. Bipolar patients can be psychotic or suicidal. They can also be brilliant and creative.* |
| *depression* | *Characterized by the inability to respond to stimuli, by low initiative, and sullen, despondent attitudes, hopelessness and despair* |
| *treatment rates* | *Bipolar disorder and depression have higher treatment success rates than does schizophrenia* |

# — Appendix 3 —
# Note-Taking: The Split-Screen Method, a Variation on the Cornell System

Split-screen note-taking features two columns; it is especially useful for comparing/contrasting or listing pros and cons.

*Public Speaking*

*Tues., July 10*

*10 a.m.*

*Effective Note-Taking*

| From Texts | From Lecture |
|---|---|
| • always read with a pencil in hand | • sit front and center |
| • use consistent, personalized symbols to denote ideas | • use loose-leaf paper (or perforated, not spiral-bound) |
| w/which you agree | • date notes and number pages |
| w/which you disagree mentioned in class | • keep separate notes for separate classes |
| that echo the reading | • write legibly |
| that contradict assigned reading | |
| that confuse | • use a system (Précis, etc.) |
| that are controversial | • use abbrev. |
| that echo your own experience | • more is better than less |
| • predict and question before reading; then read for answers | • review each day's notes before leaving class; fill in gaps |
| • write out answers as you find them | • write a one-sentence summary of each day's main idea |
| • mark up the margins of your text | • compare with a classmate; ask your instructor to review |

# — Appendix 4 —
# Note-Taking:
# The Informal Outline

The informal outline is perhaps the most popular method of note-taking for college students. Indentation and numbers are used to group information, visually separating ideas of equal importance from ideas of lesser importance.

*English Lit.*

*Wed., Jan. 15*

*3 p.m.*

Genres: Types of Prose Writing

*1) Expository Prose = "Expository" from "Expose" (To show)*
   *a. Informs*
   *b. Evaluates*
   *c. Persuades*
   *Essays and articles are usually expository; often they have a thesis or a central point.*

*1) Narrative Prose = "Narrative" from "Narrate" (To tell)*
   *a. Biography*
      *autobiography/memoir*
      *historical*
   *b. Fiction*
      *short stories*
      *novels*
   *Can be either fact-based or fiction; narratives tell stories.*

*Concurrence: These two forms (1 and 2) can frequently be found in the same written work.*

# — Appendix 5 —
# Note-Taking:
# The Mapping Method

The mapping method is great for visual learners. In this method notes are "mapped out" visually, with the central idea or lecture topic in the center and supporting ideas and details radiating out from the center.

*Art History*

*Tues., Sept. 20*

*10 a.m.*

*Color Theory*
*(Daylight is the presence of all colors/hue)*

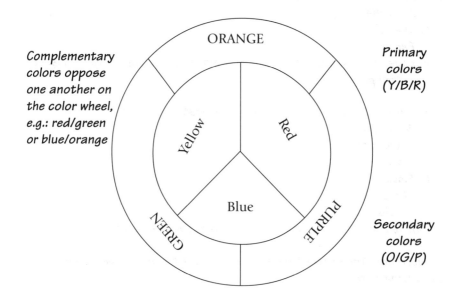

Complementary colors oppose one another on the color wheel, e.g.: red/green or blue/orange

Primary colors (Y/B/R)

Secondary colors (O/G/P)

ORANGE

Yellow

Red

Blue

GREEN

PURPLE

*A prism fragments white light into a visible spectrum*
*The order of the visible spectrum is:*
*Red/Orange/Yellow/Green/Blue/Purple*

# — Appendix 6 —
# Note-Taking:
# The Précis Method

The précis method of note-taking features a series of précis, or summaries, of important ideas.

*American History*

*Tues., Sept. 11*

*2 p.m.*

*USA nation-building*
*From 1870 to 1914, America saw a huge increase in the size of cities, and the rate of immigration.*

*Causes of late 1800s urban growth*
*New railroads linked mining and manufacturing centers; with more jobs available, cities grew. New farm machinery slowed the need for farm labor; an economic downturn in 1873 hit farmers hard. Finally, a dramatic increase in immigration swelled American cities.*

*How immigrants helped build the USA*
*Immigrants from 1885 to 1914 came mostly from eastern and southern Europe. They worked in factories, often for low wages (sweatshops). They sent word of the "promise of America" to friends and family back home, thus spreading American ideas and spurring additional immigration.*

*Changes in American life due to urban growth*
*Museums, theaters, concert halls, electric lights, indoor plumbing—all transformed urban areas into cultural centers of the Gilded Age. Slums grew, too, as did opportunities for women's employment, labor unions, local gov't, and corruption in local gov't.*